Christmas
ON THE
HOME
FRONT

MIKE BROWN

SUTTON PUBLISHING

First published in 2004 by
Sutton Publishing Limited . Phoenix Mill
Thrupp . Stroud . Gloucestershire . GL5 2BU

British Library Cataloguing in Publication Data
A catalogue record for this book is available from the British Library.

ISBN 0-7509-3819-6

Front endpaper: Christmas party for Deptford children, 1943. *(Lewisham Local Studies)*
Back endpaper: Kings Cross underground canteen, 1944. *(London Transport Museum)*

Typeset in 12.5pt Garamond
Typesetting and origination by
Sutton Publishing Limited.
Printed and bound in England by
J.H. Haynes & Co. Ltd, Sparkford.

Contents

Acknowledgements

I would like to take this opportunity to thank the following people who so kindly shared their memories with me: Grace D., Dorothy Adcock, Arnold Beardwell, John Bird, Jackie Burns, Margaret Cordell, Margaret Cushion, Jenny D'Eath, Brenda Dudley, Bryan Farmer, Paul Fincham, Georgina Foord, Raymond Gibbons, Robina Hinton, Mrs Elizabeth Hobson, Mrs Janet Houghton, Doreen Isom, Doreen Last, Joan Letts, Roy Littler, Nita Luce, Norman Mallins, Brian Martin, Patricia McGuire, John Middleton, Sybil Morley, Grace Newman, Grace Newsom, Mike Owen, Margaret Peers, Wendy Peters, Yvonne Pole, Roy Proctor, Ernie Prowse, Betty Quiller, Lily Roberts, Doreen Robinson, Vera Rooney, Mrs Sewell, Vera Sibley, L.E. Snellgrove, Margaret Spencer, Eric Stevens, Les Sutton, Mrs B.W. Thomson (who kindly loaned the photograph on page 134), Mrs C. Thomson, Elizabeth Toy, W.J. Wheatley, Edith Wilson, Mrs D. Wilkins and Donald Wood.

Photographs: Associated Press 76, Crown Copyright 44, Empics 104, Hulton Archive/Getty Images 97, Lewisham Local History Unit 160, London Metropolitan Archives 4, 31, London Transport Museum 73, 165, N.I. Syndication 20, *Radio Times* 58, 69 99.

Photographs and illustrations from contemporary publications: *Aero Modeller* 122, *The Beano* (courtesy of D.C. Thompson & Co. Ltd) 39, *Columbia Record Guide* 158, *Daily Herald* 176, *Daily Mirror* 80, *Film Pictorial* 153, *Gifts You Can Make Yourself* 177, 178, *Good Housekeeping* 47, *Home Notes* 33, *Illustrated* 125, *Kent Messenger* 51, *Landgirl* 162, *Motor*

Cycling 107, 132, 138, *Needlewoman & Needlecraft* 124, *Punch* 92, *Sunday Dispatch* 38, 41, *Woman & Home* 45, 54, *Woman's Own* 17, *Women's Pictorial* 13, *Woman's Weekly* 156.

Finally I should like to thank the following people who have been so helpful to me: Nina Burls of the Royal Air Force Museum, Hendon, Ben Howard of the Sayers Croft Evacuation Group, and Matthew Ray of the Shaftesbury Society, my editor Clare Jackson, and as ever, William, Ralph and Carol.

Introduction

The nation has made a resolve that, war or no war, the children of England will not be cheated out of the one day they look forward to all year. So, as far as possible, this will be an old-fashioned Christmas in England, at least for the children.

Ministry of Information short film, Christmas under Fire *(1940)*

When war broke out in September 1939 it was not uncommon, once again, to hear the remark, 'It'll all be over by Christmas!' Actually there would be six Christmases before it really was 'all over', and in the interim the war would bring about the disappearance of many traditional British festivals. Guy Fawkes' night went immediately: all gunpowder production was needed for the war effort and bonfires contravened the blackout. Summer holidays became a thing of the past in 1940 as total war, and Lord Beaverbrook, demanded ever-increasing production. Easter eggs became rare when sugar was rationed and disappeared altogether with sweet rationing. This left Christmas.

One of the biggest problems encountered in any attempt to study Britain during the war can be summed up in the phrase 'regional variations'. Make any statement about food or Civil Defence and you will receive a barrage of responses along the lines of 'it wasn't like that where I was!' The availability of food, for example, varied tremendously, with the countryside generally faring much better than the towns, and for many, mainly in the towns and cities, bombing was a common experience, whereas some rural areas never saw an enemy bomber. Some people saw it

WAR OR NO WAR

Here's that man again!

Dashing about in the black-out he's busier than ever. Rarely has he been more welcome, with his load of Electric Gifts.

Visit the Electricity Showrooms and make your choice.

Showrooms :

HIGH STREET, LEWISHAM, S.E.13.
Telephone : LEE Green 5001-10
SYDENHAM ROAD, SYDENHAM, S.E.26.
Telephone : SYDenham 8763
11, STRATHEDEN PARADE, BLACKHEATH, S.E.3.
Telephone : GREenwich 2900
BROMLEY ROAD, DOWNHAM.
Telephone : HITher Green 2692
HIGH STREET PENGE, S.E.20.
Telephone : SYDenham 6822
South East Area Office 151-5, HIGH STREET, LEWISHAM.
Telephone : LEE GREEN 5001-10

The SOUTH METROPOLITAN ELECTRIC LIGHT & POWER COMPANY LIMITED.

as their patriotic duty to follow all the rules and advice issued by the government, while others took a far more fatalistic view: eat, drink and be merry for tomorrow we die! Christmas, however, was one of the few unifying experiences of the war: a festival that was celebrated throughout Britain, in the towns and the countryside, and by rich and poor alike. True, in Scotland as a whole, Hogmanay was a far more important event, probably more so even than today, yet Christmas was also celebrated.

It also has to be remembered that the divide between rich and poor was much bigger in the 1930s and '40s. Make do and mend was, for many families, nothing new; only the middle and upper classes saw such scrimping as a patriotic wartime duty. For many others it had always been a way of life. And we should not overlook the fact that the home-front experience changed as the war went on. Christmas, as a regular fixed event, throws into vivid contrast the changes which happened during the five years of war.

Of course, wartime Christmases need to be looked at from the perspective of their 1930s predecessors: there were fewer presents, a much shorter run up and holiday, and goose was still the traditional main dish. Mike Owen remembers: 'On Christmas morning Mother would have been up at 6am to begin the preparation of the goose. The pudding took several hours of steaming, the kitchen walls would drip with condensation.'

To demonstrate how Christmas changed over the course of the war the book is divided into six main chapters covering consecutive years. Each of the first five chapters also includes a section on a particular topic, such as wartime weddings and Christmas among the evacuees.

ONE

The First Wartime Christmas

Christmas 1939 was in many ways like a pre-war Christmas. There were, of course, emergency restrictions in place that affected the seasonal festivities, particularly the blackout regulations which made the traditional sight of Christmas trees decked with coloured lights, glimpsed through street windows, a thing of the past. One advert ran: 'As dusk falls, the fairy lights on the Christmas tree outside St Paul's Cathedral will go out . . . we must await Victory to again see them at night in all their colours.' The delights of Christmas shopping were somewhat muted as the classic Yuletide shop window displays were unlit by night and obscured by anti-blast tape by day. Shopkeepers complained loudly that the blackout restrictions were curtailing trade, and on 2 December the Ministry of Home Security approved a device to help them. It took the form of a light in a special container, which threw its illumination either up or down and inwards, illuminating shop window displays without casting reflections in the street.

Window-shopping wasn't the only thing affected by the blackout. In the four months between the outbreak of war and the first wartime Christmas around 4,000 civilians were killed on the roads, compared with just 2,500 for the corresponding period in 1938. And this was despite petrol rationing. On 3 September it had been announced that each motorist would be allowed between 4 and 10 gallons of petrol a month, depending on the horsepower of their car, beginning in that month. In December accidents claimed 1,155 lives, the highest figure since records were kept. In Birmingham the number of accidents was up by 81 per cent, while in

CHRISTMAS DAY BLACKOUT TIMES

London	5.23 p.m.	to	8.37 a.m.	Leeds	5.18 p.m. to	8.54 a.m.
Aberdeen	4.58		9.18	Liverpool	5.26	8.59
Belfast	5.31		9.17	Newcastle	5.11	9.02
Birmingham	5.26		8.49	Penzance	5.51	8.53
Bristol	5.33		8.47	Plymouth	5.47	8.46
Cardiff	5.37		8.48			
Edinburgh	5.11		9.14			
Glasgow	5.16		9.19			

These were the precise times given for 1940 and 1943, but in other years there was little variation.

Glasgow the figure trebled. The government, however, remained adamant that this was all the fault of stupidly careless pedestrians.

During the 'Phoney War' the blackout was a constant reminder to the civilian population that Britain was at war.

Money was tight. In order to raise the £2 billion towards the cost of the war, the Chancellor, Sir John Simon, had introduced his War Budget on 27 September. This raised the standard rate of tax from 5s 6d to 7s 6d in the pound, at the same time reducing the married man's allowance and imposing a 10 per cent increase in estate duty. It was expected that, for the nation's sake, everyone would grin and bear increases of 1d a pint on beer, 1s 6d a bottle on whisky, 1d a packet on cigarettes, 2s per lb on tobacco, and 1d per lb on sugar, with the cost of all these increases being borne entirely by the consumer. All trades benefiting from the war were to pay an excess profits tax of 60 per cent; this was partly in response to the public outcry at the huge price increases that had quickly followed the declaration of war, and partly in an attempt to crack down on the type of profiteering that had been rife in the First World War. Actually, after an initial steep rise the prices of most goods had quickly fallen again, almost back to normal, but as an extra guarantee the Chancellor undertook to subsidise certain essential commodities, such as bread, flour, meat and milk, in order to keep down prices. Yet in spite of this, the various tax rises meant hefty cuts in the amount of disposable income available to most, even for teetotal non-smokers.

The weather was very seasonal. Most of Britain, indeed much of western Europe, was carpeted in deep snow during a very cold December, which was followed by the coldest January in Britain for nearly half a century. An 8-mile stretch of the River Thames froze between Teddington and Sunbury, and the Serpentine Swimming Club's annual Christmas morning handicap had to be postponed as 'there was too much ice to permit the holding of a race under fair conditions'. Ada Pope of Margate described how 'the frost made the country look like a Christmas card', while William Dudley wrote:

> It was cold. Frogs in ice-bound pools were having a cushy time compared with us. All brass monkeys were carefully transported inside and kept near the fire. The trees bore a load of ice. Even the grass stems were icicles. And to add to it all there was a fuel shortage.

The war news was good. The universally expected and much-feared mass raids by Göring's *Luftwaffe* had failed to materialise; rather than the hundreds of thousands of deaths that had been anticipated, in fact, by Christmas not a single British civilian had been killed by enemy bombing. What little German air activity there was, had been confined to Scotland; during December there had been attacks along the Firth of Forth on the 7th and the 22nd. There had also been some mine-laying activities around the south and east coasts of England.

Winter 1939 was the coldest for nearly fifty years, with widespread blizzards. These London evacuees are making the most of the snow in Hastings, January 1940. (*Courtesy of London Metropolitan Archives*)

Much of the foreign war news concerned the small Finnish army's stout defence against their vastly superior Russian opponents, but the newspapers also covered the arrival of various Commonwealth troops. There were flight crews from New Zealand, and troops from Cyprus (who had arrived in France), while in the week before Christmas the papers described the arrival of the first Canadian troops in Britain. At sea the Royal Navy was fighting in the Battle of the Atlantic: on 17 December the crew of the *Graf Spee*, one of Germany's new pocket battleships, had chosen to scuttle its vessel in Montevideo harbour rather than face the pursuing British ships.

For many households the Christmas celebrations were muted by the fact that so many people were absent. Fathers, brothers and sons were all serving their country somewhere in France: indeed, almost ½ million men were on active service by Christmas 1939. Sybil Morley's father was the rector of a very scattered country parish in Essex, about 7 miles from Colchester, a garrison town. She recalled:

> Early wartime Christmases were spent surrounded by soldiers – there was an invitation to them to come and spend Christmas afternoon with us. We always went to church first of course, and we children were allowed to take one present with us.
>
> In the afternoon the soldiers arrived. Some came by taxi, some cycled and some even walked. They all seemed to enjoy being in someone's home, chatting and eating whatever my mother could provide for them.

The government was keen that this should be a happy Christmas, in spite of the war. With puritanical zeal cinemas, theatres and other sources of entertainment had been shut down or had their opening hours restricted in the first few days of the war, but this was soon seen as a morale-sapping disaster. The authorities would not make the same mistake about Christmas; of course over-indulgence was to be discouraged, but people needed to know what they were fighting for, and Christmas, with all that it implied about tradition, family values, faith, neighbourliness, community, even peace on earth, was just the thing. Magazines, newspapers and radio articles all stressed the point.

In an article in *Woman's Own* on 23 December Rosita Forbes argued that making this a good Christmas was almost a duty:

Remember there are lots and lots of happy Christmases ahead. You can be utterly sure of that . . . We're all working, you see, for the same great purpose and it is just as much as a crusade – against nations which have no use for Christmas because they have 'abolished God' – as that which Christ fought for us . . . Your faith, your laughter and your certainty of good in the end, can make this Christmas as happy as any other . . . There is only one front. We're manning it shoulder to shoulder. When the war is won, the effort of every woman – yours and mine and your neighbour's – will have contributed to the victory . . . Let's have all the ammunition for the Christmas front that we can afford.

But not everyone was in the mood for a happy Christmas. The editorial of the *Guider* magazine that December began:

So many people have said to me lately that they could not bring themselves to think of Christmas, not only because, this year, for many of us Christmas must be a reminder of other happier times, not only because many of us will be alone among strangers, separated from our families, anxious about people we love who may be in danger, but for a bigger, more unselfish reason. They cannot bear to think of Christmas because this year so much that they believed in has been broken.

Woman's Own addressed the point about absent friends and family:

Are you looking forward to Christmas? Yes I know, in some ways it's going to be awfully different; but it is going to be Christmas perhaps more than ever before . . . For instance, I expect a good many of you won't be able to see the people who matter most to you this Christmas-time. And there'll be a corner in your heart that has an ache in it – but 'he' or 'she' or 'they' whom you miss have it too, and that brings you closer together. And you are both determined to make Christmas as cheery as possible for the people you do see.

As yet there was no food rationing. Many people remembered the serious shortages that had developed in the First World War, and there was general concern about profiteering. At first there were a few shortages, which the government addressed by a scheme known as 'pooling'. All supplies of certain items such as petrol and butter had to be put into a 'pool', and sold as a single, and therefore more controllable, product, using names such as 'national butter'. Some people had already begun hoarding various items, and the government was not quite sure how to react to this. Certainly, if people were to lay down a small store of food to counter any future disruption of supply this would, within reason, be a good thing, as it would help to minimise the disruption caused. Yet at the same time over-storing would in itself cause shortages, which would bring about panic-buying and profiteering. The public were advised to lay in a small store, and were even given lists of appropriate goods, yet this could not fully control the issue. The fear of missing out, or of not providing properly for your family, especially when other people were known to be amassing large stocks, drove many who could afford it to get what they could, especially if there was a hint that this or that item would soon be unobtainable.

In October the newspapers had speculated that meat and butter would soon be rationed. Eventually the government bowed to the inevitable and on 29 November the Minister of Food, W.S. Morrison, announced that the rationing of butter and bacon would commence on 8 January, and in the meantime self-discipline and restraint were the order of the day – officially. But since people were aware that rationing would be introduced just after Christmas, few took any notice. Most took the opportunity to splurge before rationing was introduced; hotels were fully booked over the festive season, as were restaurants. *Woman's Pictorial* magazine spoke for many: 'One of the best things about Christmas is all the lovely things we have to eat – a greedy thought perhaps, but I think it is one that most people have. Why we don't have plum puddings, turkey and mince pies at other times of the year I don't know.' A Stork margarine advertisement from that Christmas read: 'What if there is a war on? Christmas parties mustn't be called off on that

DECEMBER 9, 1939

Cecile's New Series

CHRISTMAS PUDDING

An Economical One—But Very Delicious

INGREDIENTS

Quarter of a pound of flour
One level teaspoonful of baking powder or use self-raising flour
One medium-sized carrot
Quarter of a pound of sugar
Quarter of a pound of currants
Two ounces of stoned raisins
Two ounces of sultanas
Four ounces of breadcrumbs
Three ounces of shredded suet
Half a level teaspoonful of ground nutmeg
Half a level teaspoonful of ground cinnamon
One egg
Milk to moisten

METHOD

WASH, pick over and dry the fruit, and stone and cut up the raisins.
Sift the flour with the baking powder and spices and mix with the shredded suet.
Add the sugar, breadcrumbs and prepared fruit, and mix all together. Stir in the grated carrot and add the whisked egg and milk to moisten.
Beat well before turning it into a well-greased basin, cover with greased paper and then a floured pudding cloth, and stand in a pan of boiling water, the latter reaching about half way up the side of the basin.
Cook for about three hours, keeping the water boiling all the time. As the water boils away, replenish with more *boiling* water.
When cooked, leave to get cold and keep in a cool, dry place until Christmas.
When required, steam for about one hour, then turn out and serve with either sweet white sauce or hot custard.

SWEET WHITE SAUCE

INGREDIENTS

Half an ounce of margarine
Half an ounce of flour
Half a pint of milk
One and a half level dessertspoonfuls of sugar
Vanilla essence

METHOD

MELT the fat in a saucepan, add the flour, and when well blended gradually stir in a quarter of a pint of the milk and bring to the boil. Stir in the remainder of the milk gradually and bring to the boil again.
Let this boil gently for a few minutes then add the sugar and stir till dissolved. Remove from the stove and add vanilla essence to taste.
Pour into a sauceboat and serve with the pudding.

VARIATIONS

GOLDEN syrup may be used to sweeten instead of sugar. If using this, warm the syrup slightly and whisk up with the egg.
If plenty of fruit is available, more may be used, including a little candied peel.
One or two more ounces of shredded suet may be added.
Mixed spice may be substituted for the cinnamon and nutmeg.
Some ale may be used to moisten instead of milk.

As yet rationing had not been introduced. Once it had, many recipes from this period would soon seem lavish. (*Woman's Weekly*)

account! There'll be your men on leave to be entertained, your National Service workers needing relaxation. And cooking won't be difficult – not now you can get Stork again, as much of it as you want.' It went on to give recipes for Christmas trifle and mince pies, using 'wartime mincemeat'.

Many Christmas recipes published in women's magazines that December would soon seem lavish as shortages and rationing began to bite. Typical of this extravagance was the recipe for Christmas pudding printed in *Woman's Weekly*. The ingredients for this included sugar, suet and margarine, all rationed in 1940, and egg, milk and dried fruit, all put on distribution schemes in 1940 and 1941. Even the breadcrumbs and flour would have to be National Wheatmeal after 1941. The following recipes, both from 1939, should be compared with ones from later in the war to show how deeply rationing was to affect Britain.

WARTIME MINCEMEAT

1lb raisins, stoned and chopped
1lb sultanas, cleaned
1lb currants, cleaned
½lb Stork margarine, melted
1lb apples, peeled and grated

1lb candied peel, chopped
2 nutmegs, grated
½lb demerara or granulated sugar
rind and juice of two lemons

Mix all the prepared fruits together, add the grated nutmeg, lemon rind and juice, and the sugar. Melt Stork and stir into the mixture. Stir well, put into clean, warm jars, and tie down securely. This quantity makes about three 2lb jars.

Stork Margarine advertisement

Woman's Own carried recipes for unboiled marzipan, with directions for making marzipan holly and fruits, jelly, Christmas pudding, iced mince pies, trifle and shortbread. They also gave instructions for a complete Christmas dinner consisting of 'clear soup, roast turkey with chestnut and forcemeat stuffing, bread sauce, baked potatoes and Brussels sprouts or celery, Christmas pudding or mince pies'.

The Christmas tree, having been introduced in Victorian times, had by now become firmly rooted (excuse the pun) in the traditional British Christmas. On the outbreak of war wood was one of the first items to suffer supply restrictions, but a spokesman for the state forests let it be known that there would be no shortage of Christmas trees that year.

Henry Bailey wrote: 'The curtains were drawn and the fairy lamps at the top of the Christmas tree were the only lights. Their red, blue, yellow and green hues shone out and glistened on the tinsel and the silver bells, and it looked very nice in the dark.' By now strings of coloured electric lights were available, though many people still used candles. Maureen Salmon wrote: 'Our nursery looked lovely with trails of ivy and holly and with lighted Chinese lanterns.'

A few of the products that were available in late 1939 would soon disappear altogether. For example, some companies were still advertising indoor fireworks that year. Ernie Prowse recalled:

HOW TO MAKE THE PERFECT CHRISTMAS CAKE

10oz butter
12oz Barbados sugar
6 eggs
13oz plain flour
1 teaspoon Borwick's baking powder
1 teaspoon mixed spice
1 tablespoon black treacle

2oz ground almonds
4oz chopped almonds
1¾lb currants
14oz sultanas
10oz mixed peel
grated rind and juice of ½ lemon and ½ orange
wineglassful rum or brandy (optional)

Cream the butter and sugar together. Mix in the eggs and treacle very thoroughly. Add the sifted dry ingredients, the fruit, almonds, lemon and orange juice and rind. Also brandy. Put the mixture into a well greased and lined tin, and bake in a cool oven for six hours (temp 275°), lessen oven heat after two hours. Keep two or three weeks, then cover with almond paste about half an inch thick and ice with royal icing.

For the almond paste mix 3oz each of castor sugar and ground almonds together. Add half a teaspoonful of almond essence and sufficient egg to make fairly soft consistency. Work till smooth and roll out. Cover over cake.

For the royal icing, beat the whites of two eggs lightly and add two teaspoons lemon juice. Gradually beat in 1lb icing sugar till mixture keeps its shape when dropped from spoon. Use immediately, keeping well covered with a damp cloth when in the basin to prevent hardening. Spread over cake with a long knife dipped in cold water. Decorate to suit.

Borwick's Baking Powder advertisement

Auntie Win always had a lot of Christmas fireworks which must have cost a lot of money. One in particular stays with me; it was a round black thing about two inches high with a touch paper. When you lit it, it would start off with smoke coming out, then it would suddenly send out a long black snake-like thing which would go on for a long time. In the end it would be about three feet long. The only problem was it would give off a lot of smoke and really stink!

Although many people still used candles on trees – indeed in some areas there was no mains electricity – electric tree sets were available, as this advert from the pre-war 'Slonetric' catalogue shows.

Paul Fincham recalled:

> There was still a good deal of pre-war sort of stuff around. I'd been sent to stay with friends of my parents in Norfolk from September until just before Christmas. I well remember going to do my Christmas shopping at Woolworth's in Diss before going home to my parents, and you could buy almost anything that you'd have bought in peacetime. I bought, for 6d, a box of those tiny crackers to put on a Christmas tree, and a packet of paper napkins, also 6d, and similar things.

Indoor fireworks were one of the party treats available that year, but like much else, they were soon to disappear.

An advertising campaign encouraged people to buy French food and drink, Alsatian wines, kirsch, cognac, cheeses and the like. One of the more bizarre aspects of that first wartime Christmas was that so many of the troops with the British Expeditionary Force in France, especially the officers, received parcels from home packed with the sort of French produce they themselves could buy in the local shops.

Woman's Own had its own suggestions:

> There's a lot we can do to cheer the troops . . . For instance, here's an idea for mothers and sweethearts and wives who've already heaped the usual home comforts on their particular bit of the Forces. You know it's far more difficult for the authorities to keep the boys from getting bored in their time off than it is to supply food and clothing. So *Woman's Own* has arranged for the two main male hobbies – reading and darts – to be carried on even in the most obscure trench in the lines.

We'll send to any address you like to give a parcel containing super Christmas numbers of five men's magazines, a set of darts in a case and a charming little Christmas card bearing your name – all for 3s 6d.

Woman's Pictorial suggested various presents for servicemen:

Of course, you can do other things but knit for your man. Send him his favourite boiled sweets, or jam, biscuits, chutney, plum cake, either that you have made him or bought for him. . . . You know there will be times when he is billeted in a village or in reach of a village, and of course you want him to do you credit among your French neighbours. He can't look spruce without shaving cream, spare razor blades, and toilet soap (large tablets and not highly scented or he'll be called a cissy).

Even if he went off with your photo in his pocket, send him a new one just to show you haven't changed. Send it in a wallet where he can keep his paper money, and it's a good idea to line the wallet with jaconet as this is gas-resisting. He'd love snaps of the kiddies, the dog, the house under snow and the first chrysanthemums in the garden, too. . . . And now a last idea. On Christmas Day save one of everything from the table. A mince pie,

Many adverts suggested presents for family members in the forces, and many mothers then, as today, worried that their absent sons might fail to keep clean – as if the Sergeant Major would have allowed that!

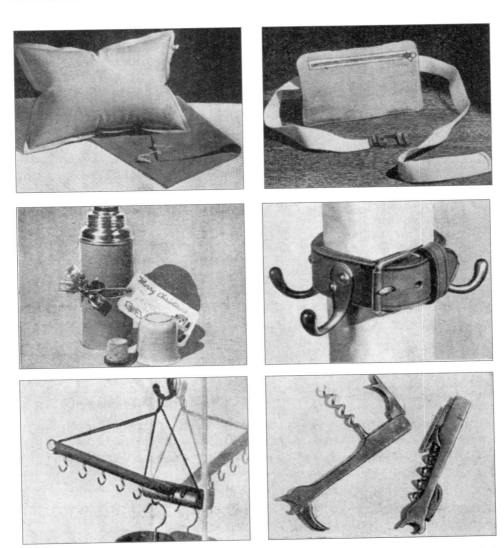

A range of gift suggestions for men in the forces from a *Women's Pictorial* article, 'What shall we give them?', which reflect the rather quaint view of the war prevalent at the time.

a piece of Christmas Cake, a motto from a cracker (see that it's a nice one), a ribbon from your dress – and send it to him just to show you were thinking about him and wishing he were with you.

There was some dispute in the government over whether a little extra spending that Christmas would be a good thing; several said it was

" You're *quite* sure it's a *balaclava* helmet ?   He's so *frightfully* particular . . ."

David Langdon's humorous view of the difficulties of buying gifts for troops. The cold winter meant that a balaclava helmet would be a most welcome gift.

good for morale, whereas the Chancellor, Sir John Simon, insisted that money should not be 'wasted' on presents. Others took the view that spending was patriotic – armchair economists pointed out that the war would be paid for through indirect taxation if every adult smoked two packets of cigarettes and drank half a bottle of whisky a day!

Various 'economical' presents were suggested, including this, from *Woman's Own*: 'If you have been able to plant bulbs in time for Christmas – you'll be able to give some of your friends the loveliest gift on earth.' Also, 'Half-crown gifts can look like a guinea if you take a little trouble with them. For instance, a gay sixpenny posy makes a two-shilling puff look really elegant – while two quarter-yard lengths of cleverly contrasting georgette [sewn back-to-back] make a very chic and exclusive-looking scarf.'

According to the *Guider* magazine:

This year we must have an economy Christmas, but we do not want to lose the festive spirit and many Guides will be planning Christmas presents in spite of the war. Not only are there families and friends to plan for, but this year there are many evacuated children who appreciate presents from Guides. Here are some suggestions for making presents out of old pieces of material as well as new for grown-ups and children.

The article went on to give instructions for creating 'soft toys': 'Guides who have had experience making felt toys can start to collect pieces of old grey flannel for elephants, old tweed coats for horses, old felt or velour hats for rabbits, and set to work with the aid of Craft Council patterns to make something out of nothing.' A selection of patterns cost 1s, while packets containing everything necessary to make the toy cost from 1s 2d to 2s 6d. These included Paul the Polar Bear, Hengist the Horse and Dackie the Dachshund. (It is interesting that the irrational hatred shown by the public towards German dogs during the First World War hardly existed now.) Better still were:

> Rubber Toys. Floating toys, in the shape of fishes, seahorses and other aquatic creatures, for the bath, can be made out of old inner tubes of tyres or hot water bottles (the latter should be used for small toys only). They are cut out with scissors and stuck together with rubber solution – the same sort which is used to mend bicycle tyres. They are stuffed with kapok or chopped up bits of rubber or cork sawdust from fruit packing.

Patterns available included Polly the Plaice, Charles the Crocodile, and Monty the Mackerel, price 1d each.

The *Guider* magazine also had other ideas: 'For grown-ups: Gas Mask Cases. A gas mask is not a very Christmassy object, but it can be far more cheerful if it is in a pretty case. One made from a Craft Council packet – either a plain cover for the standard box, or a decorated felt sack with a zip fastener – would make a sensible Christmas present which is quite easy to make.' The pattern for the standard case cost 1d, the packet 7d, while the packet for the felt sack with zip cost 1s 9d.

For those who could afford it, popular gifts for children included uniforms: nurse, Red Cross, pilot officer, and naval officer at 5s 11d each, while for older children a tin helmet was most welcome. Other toys included the traditional boy's favourite – a fort. Most popular were modern variations: small versions of the Maginot line with underground quarters and pill-boxes and a large turret with a revolving cupola containing a field gun. John Bird remembers 'looking in toy-shop windows and wondering how I could raise the cash for a model barrage balloon complete with winch and cables, costing about eight shillings. Unfortunately Father Christmas never heard my plea!'

There were also many topical games available, including card games such as 'Blackout', or 'Vacuation', and numerous children's annuals were produced. 'Give books this Christmas and forget the war', exhorted the *Guider*. Brian Martin recalled:

> I was 8 years old when war broke out and I had just started to have a Meccano set as the main present, a set being added each year to convert No. 1 into No. 2, etc. War stopped this so I was given a balsa-wood flying scale model kit to make up, cutting spars, stringers and moulding propellers. The kits were by Astral. In 1942 the Stirling giant bomber with 38-inch wingspan cost 21s. At these prices you can see why this would have to be the main present. Over the years I had a Stirling, Bristol Blenheim, Hampden, Whitley and Lysander.

Topical gifts for adults included Bakelite helmets, and gas-mask cases in 'neat Morocco and calf grained patent Leathercloth' for 2s. There was also a range of 'shelter-goods', including siren suits (known as shelter suits at the time) and the 'Take coverlet' – a sort of cross between a sleeping bag and an overcoat, which almost allowed you to walk to the shelter without getting out of bed. Another must-have article was the personal gas-proof suit in coloured oil silk, which cost £2, weighed in at just 4oz and offered protection from mustard gas for 'three-quarters of an hour'.

Less topical presents included the usual peacetime fare of perfume, cosmetics, soap, cigarettes, cigars and, of course, drink. Soon all these would be very difficult to obtain, but in December 1939 few could foresee this. Luxury goods in vogue included mink ties at up to 50 guineas each.

One complaint about buying presents that winter, as with much else, was profiteering. The *Daily Mirror* reported the following:

Woman's Own, December 23, 1939

FOR GIRL FRIENDS

These smart accessories are amusing to knit, would make splendid presents and might use up odd ounces

Homemade gifts 'for girl friends', from *Woman's Own*, 23 December 1939.

With Christmas only a few weeks away you will be buying toys soon. When you do, see that you don't have the same trouble as Mrs Clough of Gordon Road, Nelson, Lancs. A week ago Mrs Clough asked the price of a toy. It was *2s 6d*. A few days later she bought the toy. Its price had jumped to *2s 11d*.

It was from new stock that had just come in, the shopkeeper explained when Mrs Clough protested against the fivepence increase. And he might have got away with it had Mrs Clough been less observant. For on the box was a 'Made in Germany' label.

'This is rubbing it in with a vengeance,' said Mrs Clough. 'We have German goods pushed on to us and an unwarranted increase in price into the bargain.'

Most people celebrated Christmas at home. All television broadcasting in Britain had ceased on 1 September, and the vast majority who listened to the radio also had their enjoyment severely curtailed when the BBC's output of eight regional stations was reduced to a single national station, the Home Service.

BBC Christmas Day programmes 7.00 a.m. – 2.15 p.m.

7.00:	*Christmas Greetings* – a sackful of stories, verses and records
7.40:	The Reginald King Trio
8.15:	Christmas Carols
8.40:	*Christmas Gifts for the Children*, by the Caravan Players
9.00:	*Christmas and the Flying Angel*, a Christmas Day broadcast from the Sailors' Mission, Swansea
9.30:	Choral Mass by the St John Lateran Choir
10.00:	*Bethlehem*, a nativity play by Bernard Walker
10.30:	The Bernard Cook Quintet
10.55:	A Christmas Morning Service from the Chapel Royal, St James's Palace
12.00:	Foden's Motor Works Band
12.30:	Three Stories by Algernon Blackwood
1.10:	An Orchestral Concert conducted by Guy Warrack
1.35:	*The Soldier Sings*, a programme of national and popular songs
2.15:	*The Empire's Greeting*. 'On Christmas Day . . . when most people at home will be nearing the end of their Christmas dinners, the sound of Christmas bells will ring out from all the home and overseas transmitters of the BBC. Across the five continents and the seven seas London will be calling, sending Christmas greetings throughout the world.'

In The Empire's Greeting, messages were received from a Royal Navy destroyer, from the soldiers of the BEF in France, from an airborne RAF aircraft, from London and from the West Country, 'where a farmer and his wife have two extra places at their Christmas table for two young London guests'. Then it was on to Wales to hear a miners' choir, to Northern Ireland and a shipyard worker's house, to a ceilidh on the western coast of Scotland and then to Northumbria. The programme then broadcast messages from a Newfoundland fisherman, a Canadian pilot, a farmer in New Zealand, a dressmaker in Sydney, a Malayan naval rating, an Indian

Army officer, and a member of Cape Town's Coastal Defence Service. Finally a shepherd in the Cotswolds passed on the Empire's greetings to the King. This was answered by the next broadcast at 3pm, when His Majesty the King read out his message to the Empire.

The first Christmas radio speech by the King to the people of the Empire had been broadcast by George V in 1932. After that he continued the practice every year until 1935. Edward VIII had, of course, not done so, nor in his first year as king had George VI, but in 1937, in spite of his dread of public speaking (because of his stammer), the new king had made a broadcast. He did not repeat the process in 1938 but in 1939 it was agreed that, under the circumstances, a message from the King would serve as a tremendous morale-booster for the people.

Dressed in the uniform of an Admiral of the Fleet, the King sat in front of two microphones on a table at Sandringham to broadcast his message to the people. The *Radio Times* of 8 December summed it up: 'On Christmas Day, of course, the big event is the King's broadcast in the afternoon.' The speech itself was uplifting, it included:

A new year is at hand. We cannot tell what it will bring. If it brings peace, how thankful we shall all be. If it brings us continued struggle, we shall remain undaunted.

In the meantime I feel that we may all find a message of encouragement in the lines which, in my closing words, I would like to say to you: 'I said to the man who stood at the Gate of the Year, "Give me a light that I may tread safely into the unknown." And he replied, "Go out into the darkness, and put your hand into the Hand of God. That shall be to you better than light, and safer than a known way."' May that Almighty Hand guide and uphold us all.

People all over the country listened in, quite a few of them, especially ex-soldiers, standing to attention. Henry Bailey, then in the Shaftesbury Society's Hastings Home for Crippled Boys, wrote: 'When the Christmas

King George VI, dressed in naval uniform, makes his Christmas broadcast to the Empire from his desk in Sandringham. It was so successful that it would become an annual event, still carried on today by his daughter, Queen Elizabeth II. (*The Times, London*)

pudding came in we all applauded and several of the boys found sixpences in their helping. We all pulled our bon-bons, and soon we were wearing paper hats and blowing whistles and reading mottoes. Then we listened to the Empire Broadcast and the King's speech.' The speech deeply affected its listeners. L.E. Snellgrove recalled: 'We heard the King's broadcast about talking to the man at the gate of the year, which went down well. They [had] copies of it stuck up in Montagu Burton's in the High Street.'

The broadcast was deemed so successful that the king would speak every Christmas throughout the war. By the time the war ended it had become an institution, and the monarch's Christmas speech has been an annual event ever since.

Following the King's message there was a five-minute interval, followed by:

BBC Christmas Day Programmes 3.10 p.m. – 12.15 a.m.

3.10:   Music for Christmas, a programme of varied music

4.15:   *A Competition*, sons in France against parents in England. 'Soldiers in France will join in a parlour game with their parents in a BBC studio at home.' Games included a spelling bee, a general knowledge quiz and passing the message.

5.00:   *Christmas Greetings*, Sandy Macpherson at the theatre organ

5.30:   *Hullo, Mum*, a link-up between evacuees in a Gloucestershire village and their parents in Stepney

6.00:   *Walt Disney's Silly Symphonies*

6.20:   A Soldiers' Christmas Service from France

7.00:   *A Radio Christmas Party*. 'Comedians, Christmas songs, musical games, and join-in listening to other parties elsewhere. These will include: a pill-box fort near the front line, an Army concert from one of the bases in France, a children's hospital ward, and a wartime edition of *Flying High* from an RAF hangar.'

8.30:   An appeal on behalf of the British 'Wireless for the Blind' fund

9.00:   News

9.15:   Gracie Fields in a NAAFI variety concert, organised by ENSA, from 'somewhere in France'

9.30:   *Scheherazade*, played by the BBC Symphony Orchestra

10.30:   *A Christmas Cabaret*, starring Cyril Fletcher, Helen Hill, Harry Robbins and the Cosmopolitan Four, Fred Ballerini and his Dance Band, and Jack Hylton and his Band, with June Malo, Dolly Elsie and Bruce Trent.

12.00:   News

12.15:   Close down

The *Radio Times* summed up the BBC's Boxing Day offerings:

After two such days of listening, we shall be feeling ready for a good walk on Boxing Day. Whether we shall get it is another matter, as the broadcasting plans for that day include football from the North (Sheffield Wednesday v. Chesterfield), steeplechasing at Windsor, a broadcast from the London Coliseum pantomime *Cinderella*, ITMA (which has become one of the most popular of radio entertainments), the Kentucky Minstrels, and a composite broadcast from two English pantomimes and one in Scotland. In view of all that, who cares for the blackout? Who cares if it snows?

On the outbreak of war the government had ordered the closure of all places of entertainment, fearing the likely casualties should any be bombed. But within a week the authorities had realised the importance to morale of such places and so theatres and cinemas in neutral and reception areas were allowed to open until 10 p.m., providing that a member of staff was permanently stationed to listen out for any air-raid sirens so that the audience could be warned in good time. By the third week of the war places of entertainment in danger areas were also allowed to open until 10, except in London's West End, which was limited to 6 p.m. But by the start of December even here they could also remain open until the later time.

Many predicted that the war would bring about the end of such frivolities as pantomime. Yet, once again, those who thought that humour, enjoyment and entertainment should be dispensed with 'for the duration' were to be disappointed. In spite of, or perhaps because of, the war there was a bumper crop of pantomimes and Christmas shows that year. The *Radio Times* noted:

Instead of being blacked-out the theatre is enjoying a wartime boom. One effect of this boom is that in spite of all the Demon King may say to the contrary, Cinders will still go to the Ball this Christmas. It is not really so remarkable that we shall be seeing pantomime as that we have a theatre at all. Three months ago it seemed that the curtain was down for the duration of the war. Even when the ban on theatre opening was lifted, managers shook their heads and said 'the blackout will beat us'. As for pantomime, even the optimists thought that Jack and Jill had tumbled down-hill for the last time, the theatre's trade [going] with them.

But pantomime thrived. At the London Coliseum you could see *Cinderella*, with Joan and Doris Emney; at the Newcastle Empire there was *Puss in*

Boots with George Clark; Sandy Powell was in *Babes in the Wood* at the Coventry Hippodrome; Gene Gerrard and Bobby Comber starred in *Humpty Dumpty* at the King's Theatre, Edinburgh; Arthur Askey was in *Jack and Jill* at Birmingham, while George Formby starred in *Dick Whittington* at the Leeds Empire.

However, the war, even if it was a phoney one, did make some differences. Robina Hinton recalled: 'There was no dropping-off in the audiences, though there were a lot fewer men among them. At the start of each show, the manager would go out to the front and announce that, should the air-

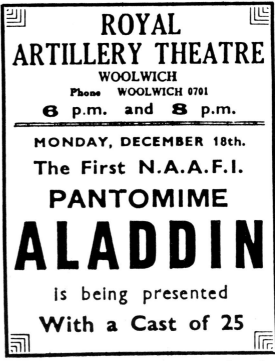

ROYAL ARTILLERY THEATRE
WOOLWICH
Phone WOOLWICH 0701
6 p.m. and 8 p.m.

MONDAY, DECEMBER 18th.
The First N.A.A.F.I.
PANTOMIME
ALADDIN
is being presented
With a Cast of 25

Many predicted that the war would see the end of pantomime, but they would soon be proved wrong – in fact it thrived.

raid warning be sounded, the audience would be informed, and they could then go to the shelter, or stay and watch the rest of the act.' Indeed, theatres were obliged to print such a notice in their programmes. The one given for the production of *Cinderella* at the Winter Garden, Drury Lane, read:

If a public air-raid warning is sounded in the course of a performance, the audience will be notified on the illuminated sign in front of the footlights. This does not necessarily mean that an air-raid will take place and we recommend you to remain in the theatre. If, however, you wish to leave, you are at liberty to do so. All we ask is that, if you feel you must go, you will depart quietly and, as far as possible, without disturbing others. The 'Raiders Passed' signal will also be shown on the illuminated sign.

As always the pantos were enlivened by songs, many of which became the hits of the period, including 'We're Going to Hang out the Washing on the Siegfried Line', 'They Can't Black Out the Moon', 'Please Leave my Butter Alone', 'Kiss me Goodnight, Sergeant-Major', 'There'll Always be an England', and 'Roll Out the Barrel'.

In *The Phoney War on the Home Front*, E.S. Turner noted that 'The Lord Chamberlain now permitted songs and jokes about Hitler. Herbert Farjeon's lyric "Even Hitler had a Mother" had been banned in 1936 and banned again with an admonition when resubmitted in 1938. It was now sanctioned.' The sheet music for 'Run Rabbit Run' was printed with alternative words, including verses such as:

> Run Adolf, run Adolf, run, run, run,
> Look what you've been and gone and done, done, done,
> We will knock the stuffing out of you;
> Field Marshal Göring and Goebbels too.
> You'll lose your place in the sun, sun, sun;
> Soon you poor dog you'll get none, none, none.
> You will flop, with Herr Ribbentrop,
> So, run Adolf, run Adolf, run, run, run.

British films on release that December included *Nurse Edith Cavell*, a real flag-waver starring Anna Neagle, Edna May Oliver and George Sanders, and *The Lion Has Wings*, starring Merle Oberon and Ralph Richardson in Alexander Korda's drama-documentary film about the pre-war RAF. For those who wanted escapist fare, there was *Cheer Boys Cheer*, a pre-Ealing British comedy about rival brewers, starring Nova Pilbeam, supported by Graham Moffatt and Moore Marriott, or George Sanders' second outing as the hero in *The Saint in London*, with Bela Lugosi as one of the baddies.

US releases included *Bridal Suite*, an MGM screwball comedy with Robert Young, and *Maisie*, starring Ann Sothern and Dick Powell, a light B-movie. This was the first of a ten-film series which would make a star of Sothern. For those who liked adventure films there was *Man of Conquest*, a biopic of the Texan hero Sam Houston, starring Richard Dix and Joan Fontaine, or *Only Angels Have Wings*, a typical Howard Hawkes' film, where men are men, starring Cary Grant, Jean Arthur, Rita Hayworth and Thomas Mitchell. For those who preferred musicals there was *Naughty but Nice*, one of Dick Powell's last musical films, with Ann Sheridan, ZaSu Pitts and Ronald Reagan (whatever happened to him?).

Much of the popular music of the period took a rather whimsical view of the war.

Alongside the main films the cinema newsreels that Christmas covered US President Roosevelt's Christmas speech, a plea for peace in which he quoted the famous biblical phrase about turning 'swords into ploughshares'. Another item featured British troops in France enjoying their Christmas dinner, or having a snowball fight in the deep snow that had settled over most of Europe, including on the front line, further enhancing the Phoney War's air of unreality. Full of smiling faces and old jokes about the sergeant major, this item was clearly an attempt to reassure anxious relatives at home that their boys were having a good time. Another such item, called *Christmas Over There*, showed British soldiers singing carols outside a French house and eating their Christmas dinner (paper hats and all) in a French barn. *With the Navy* was a similar idea for the men of the fleet. There was also a comedy item entitled *A Nasty Newsreel with Lord Haw Haw*, in which an actor impersonating William Joyce gave a comic send-up of one of his by-now familiar broadcasts.

In the 1930s, as now, Boxing Day was a big day for sport, with football, horse-racing, greyhound racing and many smaller local events, such as the annual Richmond Boxing Day Regatta. Football was the most popular spectator sport, and at the beginning of the war it had been hit by the same ban as the theatre and cinemas. Even when this was relaxed, big problems remained as the difficulties of travelling meant that the normal practice of large crowds of supporters following their team all around the country could not possibly continue. Instead the Football Association announced at the end of September that a series of regional leagues would be set up, with matches taking place only on Saturdays and public holidays. Crowd numbers were to be limited to 8,000, or 15,000 for grounds with a capacity of 60,000. Of course the nature of these new leagues meant that there was no promotion or relegation between them. There would also be no FA Cup competition 'for the duration', leaving Portsmouth, the 1939 winners, to retain the cup. *The Times* of 23 December reported:

At normal Christmas-tides the programmes of matches are of especial interest as the football season is sufficiently far advanced for the questions of the Championship, of promotion, and of relegation, to become of some urgency. This year no club will be either promoted or relegated, and the honours in football – and they are very considerable ones – will go to the teams which have the sense to realise the opportunities the unnatural circumstances give them. It is true that attendances at regional matches have been disappointing, but it is also true that those who have the football eyes to see have rejoiced in games which have been fought out with a regard for the basic principles of the game.

Attendances *were* low. That day, 23 December, one of the larger crowds, of just 5,000, saw Leeds beat Middlesbrough 3–1 in the North Eastern League. Of course, the bad weather also discouraged many spectators: the Tottenham Hotspurs v. Southend United game had already racked up three goals apiece when it was abandoned after 60 minutes due to fog.

Christmas Day saw forty-three matches, including the Glasgow Cup Final, where Rangers beat Queen's Park 3–1. South of the border, at Millwall v. Tottenham Hotspurs, one of the day's biggest crowds (7,219) watched Millwall win 5–1, while Brentford beat the FA Cup winners Portsmouth 4–0 in the South B league. There were some unusual teams out: Plymouth Argyll, for example, beat the Torpedo Depot by 5–1. On Boxing Day there were forty-one matches, including a Football League XI v. an All British XI at Wolverhampton Wanderers' ground, with proceeds going to the Red Cross (the Football League XI won 3–2). Less familiar teams playing that day included New Brighton, South Liverpool, Clapton Orient and Bournemouth & Boscombe Athletic (at that point leaders of the South B league).

Both rugby disciplines were badly hit by the war. There were thirteen Christmas Day rugby league matches, including teams from Bramley, Broughton Rangers and Liverpool Stanley, and a similar number on Boxing Day. In rugby union there were just two matches on Christmas Day – Neath beating Swansea 13–8 and Bridgend losing to Aberavon 18–3, while on Boxing Day there were eleven matches, including United Hospitals against J.G.W. Davies' Nondescripts (6–13), and two army XVs, one against Bristol (losing 23–3) and the other against Saracens (losing 10–0).

Those who enjoyed a day at the races had little choice of venue. Boxing Day meetings were limited to Windsor in England and Limerick and Leopardstown in Ireland. *The Times'* racing correspondent reported on the former: 'There was a very large attendance of visitors, one of the largest, if indeed not quite the largest, that I have seen at a Windsor jumping meeting. The going was very dead after the recent frost and mist. Runners, however, were plentiful and the afternoon's racing was most interesting and enjoyable in spite of a cold and damp afternoon.'

Traditionally greyhound racing had taken place at night, with the floodlighting adding to the excitement, but the blackout had put a stop to that. Similarly, speedway racing, another popular sport in the thirties, had

The best course this Christmas

Four grand meetings at WEST HAM over the Christmas period to cater for London's racegoers

TO-DAY   December 21st, at 1.15 p.m.
WEDNESDAY December 27th, at 1.15 p.m.
THURSDAY December 28th, at 1.15 p.m.
SATURDAY December 30th, at 1.15 p.m.

★ *Every Saturday during January "Double Session" Meetings commencing at 11.30 a.m.*
16 RACES

MEETINGS TO-DAY & ON WEDNESDAY, THURSDAY & SATURDAY of next week at 1.15 p.m.

WEST HAM STADIUM

The blackout had put a stop to open-air, floodlit events such as greyhound racing, but the stadiums responded by staging afternoon meetings, which thrived.

been run under the same conditions; failure to adjust to the ban on evening meetings, combined with the problems of petrol rationing, virtually killed off the sport at this time. In contrast, 'the dogs' responded quickly, and most successfully, to the problem. That Boxing Day there were numerous meetings throughout the day. Both Wimbledon and Coventry staged morning and afternoon meetings, while fans could also find excitement at Walthamstow, Bristol, Dagenham, Brighton, Newport, Romford and Rochester, to name just a few. There was some disquiet about this. Betting was frowned on by some – any spare money should be going to the nation's war effort, not to the bookies (the same was said of the football pools), and daytime meetings were thought to tempt workers to take time off from work. However, surveys found that the vast majority of those attending were actually servicemen on leave, or night workers, and, as with the cinema and theatre, the authorities soon recognised the value to morale of such events. Horse-racing too came in for criticism; it attracted large crowds, often travelling in expensive cars, using up large amounts of rationed petrol, and betting large amounts of money. Such criticism was shrugged off as inverted snobbery, but the petrol jibe struck a chord – in the 1943 British film *San Demetrio, London*, about a tanker battling to get to Britain in spite of U-boat and air attacks, one of the characters comments on their eventual arrival in Britain, 'That ought to take quite a few racegoers to Newmarket!'

CHRISTMAS AMONG THE EVACUEES

The younger members of many urban families had been evacuated, although there had been a gradual drift back as a result of the inactivity of the Phoney War. Of the 700,000 children officially evacuated in September only 435,000 were still away from home by December, while as many as 90 per cent of the mothers with young children who had gone had returned by Christmas. There were many who prophesied that Christmas would see the end of the evacuation scheme; they felt that if the remaining evacuee children were allowed to come home for the holiday they would never go back, and the whole scheme, already weakened, would collapse.

There was a lot of publicity concerning two particular evacuees. The King's two daughters, Princesses Elizabeth and Margaret, having stayed in Balmoral since the outbreak of war, spent two days in London on their way to Sandringham for Christmas. The authorities were furious, as the 'Evacuation Survey' report put it, 'that the press and censorship department should have sanctioned photographs of them in London; so that there was plain excuse for saying, "There! If London wasn't completely safe, do you think the government would ever have let the princesses go back there?"'

The government fought back, urging parents to 'leave the children where they are'. Barbara Hedworth, writing in *Woman's Own*, made the point:

'What! Let my little Tommy spend Christmas without his Father and Mother? I'd walk the whole way to the country and back rather than have that happen to him.'

A pair of reproachful eyes gazed into mine as I gathered my courage and pointed out: 'Yes, I know you would do that, and more – rather than pass Christmas Day without seeing your evacuated son; only you would be making the sacrifice for your own sake, not for Tommy's. You've just told me of the nice letter you have had from the people who are caring for him, that he has grown and put on weight. Tommy is going to be all right for Christmas with his new friends, and honestly I believe you would be doing him a far greater service in sending the money you saved for his fare to the woman who is looking after him, to get him those new gum-boots she says he needs and that special train he has taken a fancy to . . .' So Mothers, please put the happiness of your children before your own this Christmas time; give them the sacrifice of your personal happiness and unless there is some definite reason why you should send for your small sons and daughters or go to see them, don't renew for them the sorrow of yet another parting.

In the event a good proportion of the evacuated children did come home for the holiday. About 50,000 of them subsequently stayed, but by January the figure in billets was still about 380,000.

Some parents went to their children instead. As a small girl Mrs Sewell was evacuated from Fulham to Guildford.

Dad was in the army so mum would come down to bring our Christmas presents to us. Presents were whatever mum could get: Plasticine, chalk and a slate, crayons and a colouring book, whatever came along. Also in the stocking we might get a threepenny piece and an apple and a plum. I remember paper sheets with a doll and clothes with tabs on which you cut out so you could change her clothes. Mum knitted clothes for us – I remember she made me a cardigan. Once she bought me a stuffed doll with a china head.

Many people had particular sympathy for children away from their parents at Christmas, and strenuous efforts were made to make up for this enforced absence. L.E. Snellgrove wrote to his evacuated friend, Mervyn

Christmas 1939 was the first away from home for thousands of evacuees, so many councils and other organisations in the reception areas tried to make things better for the evacuees by providing parties, such as this one in Eastbourne. (*Courtesy of London Metropolitan Archives*)

Haisman: 'Dear Merv, Happy New Year old bean. . . . Did you have a good Christmas? I must say I felt very sorry for you for the first time since the war began, not being at home and all that.' In some areas parties for the evacuees were laid on, and some £15,000 was raised by various sources, such as newspapers, to entertain them that Christmas.

Many foster families tried hard to make it a special Christmas for their charges. Donald Wood remembered:

Another difference the war had brought was that we had two little evacuees from Battersea billeted with us, Bobby Ovett, about six, and Raymond Watkins, about eight. The boys had our usual pillow-cases on the bed which were filled while they were asleep; their parents had left things for them which we added to.

Bobby, being the youngest, still believed in Father Christmas; Raymond seemed to think it was a joke. Thus Dad had decided to prove him wrong. So there was the inevitable mince pie and glass of sherry left out on the sitting room mantelpiece, and off went the boys to bed. Needless to say both pie and sherry disappeared, and also the fire screen was knocked over and soot was scattered around the hearth. In the morning Dad sent Raymond in to fetch something, [and] he rushed out [calling], 'Mr Wood, come quick, something's happened'.

Home Notes magazine advised its readers on ways to entertain the children:

If you have some little evacuees staying with you this Christmas in addition to your own children, you're sure to be asked for a party at some time. Here are some suggestions of games that children of all ages can play and enjoy and which you might find useful to have in mind for the great occasion.

Sweet music – Ask your guests to sit in a circle and open a small box of sweets. While music is being played as for musical chairs, the box is passed from one player to the next. Whoever is holding the box when the music stops takes a sweet and retires from the game. The box is then passed on again until everyone has had a sweet.

A new version of hunt the thimble is played by hiding small novelties under chairs and tables and all sorts of odd corners about the house. Provide three times as many as you have guests (this shouldn't prove too expensive if you make 3*d* your limit) and send your guests off to look for them. Explain that each player is entitled to three novelties, and if some of the guests fail to get their share, get the others to help in the search. They'll enjoy it.

Many inner-city evacuees from working families saw an aspect of Christmas they had not previously witnessed. Dorothy Adcock recalled:

DESIGNED TO BE WORN AT PARTIES

Patterns for dresses 'Designed to be Worn at Parties' from *Home Notes*. Making your own clothes was far more common, so the introduction of 'make do and mend' was not a novelty for many families.

'In 1939 we were evacuated to Timperley, part of Altrincham, not an ideal haven as close by were Ringway (later Manchester) airport, Broadheath, and Trafford Park, where there were many munitions and engineering factories. As evacuees we were asked to several Christmas parties and were given more presents than we had ever had before – quite a pleasant memory in fact.'

Not all evacuees were in individual billets. Early in 1939 Parliament had passed the Camps Act, setting up 50 school camps which were to be self-contained evacuated schools. One of the first to be opened was Sayers Croft Camp at Ewhurst in Surrey. In May 1940 200 boys from Catford Central and Brownhill Road Schools began their 5-year stay in the camp, accompanied by their teachers and a staff of cooks, housemaids and sewing maids.

Their menu for Christmas lunch in 1940 was impressive. It consisted of 'Porc Rôti et Farci à la mode de Sayers Croft' with 'Sauce de Pommes, Choux de Brusselles and Pommes Rôti' followed by 'Pudding de Noël à la mode de Catford, Sauce Crême, Boissons Variés.' The menu ended with the hopeful wish, 'May God guard and keep the gallant men of the Royal Navy and the Merchant Service who bring us our food.'

From Brownhill to Pitch Hill, a history of the camp produced by the Sayers Croft Old Boys' Association, records that, 'At Christmas the school staff and camp put on a pantomime-type show. Always a great success. Even the five male cooks joined in by forming a chorus line, and eyes widened at the sight of the female staff in red and green tights.' The 1940 pantomime was *The Queen of Hearts*, which included 'topical lyrics by Raymond Scannell', sung by a cast comprising 'the School and Camp Staffs and their Friends'. In 1941 the show was *Xmas Pie*, 'a review with a Christmas flavour'. This included such sketches as 'The Buggins Family Entertains', and 'A Wild-West Film', various singers, St George and the Dragon – an old Cornish play, and 'The Grand Pantomime of Cinderella', culminating in 'The Grand Finale – "Light up your face with a smile".'

Other children were billeted in large groups in country mansions and stately houses. In 1942 Margaret Cordell was among more than 100 children evacuated to Waddesdon Manor in Berkshire, which was then owned and run by the Rothschilds. Margaret wrote:

The first Christmas I can remember is 1944. Christmas afternoon, all we young children had to wait in a group in the hallway. To our left was a very long room which we then proceeded down, to where Mr and Mrs James de Rothschild sat by the fireside. A shiny piano was to our left and a large decorated Christmas tree stood in front of it. While a lady pianist played on the piano, all of us children sang Christmas carols. Afterwards, the Rothschilds treated us to a party with jelly, cakes and lemonade, which was much appreciated. I had never seen so much food on a table before.

Connie Snow wrote of her stay in a Shaftesbury Society Holiday Home:

On Christmas Eve we all hung up our stockings and in the morning, to our surprise, we found toys, sweets, and an orange each. We were all very excited for we knew that we were going to have a large Christmas tree. After eating a delicious Christmas dinner we all soon had fancy dresses on, while the nurses put the presents on the tree. Not long after we walked happily to the dining-room, where laid out on the tables was a bon-bon each and some beautiful things to eat. After a good tea we all ran into our playroom and while we were waiting for Santa Claus we were allowed to blow bubbles. Soon he came, and when he came in we all sang 'Jolly old Santa Claus'. He took the presents off the tree, and the one for me was a lovely necklace.

Gwen West was at Bognor Regis: 'We had a party after tea and played at all sorts of games. After a while we heard a knocking at the door. We thought it was an air-raid warden knocking to tell us there was a light, but Sister opened the door to find Father Christmas waiting to give us our toys. Everyone had a lovely present, and all the nurses had a present too.'

Later in the war, as the bombing subsided, more and more children began to return home for the holidays. W.J. Wheatley recalled: 'At Christmas 1942 our two schoolboy evacuees went home to Sidcup for the holidays, because the bombing of London had gone quiet for the time being. They returned to us in early January for the start of the school term.'

CHRISTMAS 1940

..there's nothing like

BIRD'S
CUSTARD

TWO

—— 1940 ——

The Second Christmas

Unlike that of 1939, 1940's really was a wartime Christmas. During the previous twelve months France, Holland, Belgium and the rest of Western Europe had been overwhelmed by the German Blitzkrieg. Thousands of British troops had been killed, wounded or taken prisoner in Norway, Belgium and France. After this had come the invasion scare and the Blitz – it seemed that nothing could stop the German advance. Indeed, many were amazed when Christmas came and Britain still survived as a nation. The coming of winter brought some respite, as the invasion was not now expected until the spring. However, not even at Christmas was the ban on the ringing of church bells to be lifted – they were *only* to be rung as a signal that enemy forces were landing. But despite the fact that there would be no bells to welcome the Christ Child that year, the churches were crowded.

The bombing continued. During the month of December targets had included Birmingham, Bristol, London, Manchester, Merseyside, Sheffield and Southampton. In all, 35,000 tons of bombs had been dropped on Britain over the year, resulting in the deaths of almost 24,000 civilians. But bombing was not the only threat. On the evening of 21 December, after a week's silence, the German long-range guns at Cap Gris Nez opened up with a 15-minute bombardment of the Dover area.

In contrast December had brought good news from overseas: the Italian attack on Greece had been withstood, and even repulsed, with British troops arriving there to support their Greek allies. In Libya too, British forces were driving back the Italians; on 11 December Sidi Barrani had fallen, and some

Christmas Greetings 1940
in this, Britain's Finest Hour
From the Manufacturers of
SMITH'S 'SECTRIC' and LEVER CLOCKS

'Britain's Finest Hour'. A very neat bit of advertising from Smiths' clocks. (*Sunday Dispatch*)

20,000 Italians were taken prisoner. The RAF was hitting back; during December they had bombed several German cities including Berlin, Bremen, Cologne, Düsseldorf, Frankfurt, Kiel, Mannheim and Wilhelmshafen. Other targets had included the invasion ports along the French coast and aerodromes in Sicily.

The weather reflected the nation's mood. Everything was grey, as most of Britain laboured under overcast, drizzle or fog. L.E. Snellgrove wrote: 'I think my memories of this Christmas will be of fog! Every time Dad and I went up to the baths it was foggy. I also said good-bye to uncle Will in the thick fog just before Christmas. He was called up and came to say good-bye to Mum and Dad . . . Being a romantic, I watched him disappear in the swirling fog thinking that it might be the last time.'

By December British shipping losses since the beginning of the war had reached 3.8 million tons, and food rationing had been a fact of everyday life for almost a year, but this would be the first Christmas 'on the ration'. By now, weekly rations were 4oz bacon and/or ham, 6oz butter and/or margarine, 2oz tea, 8oz sugar and 2oz cooking fats; meat, which was rationed by value, was reduced from 2*s* 2*d* to 1*s* 10*d* from 16 December. As a special treat, for the week before Christmas the tea ration was doubled to 4oz and sugar increased from 8 to 12oz. People were warned, however, that after Christmas further belt-tightening would be necessary.

The comics went to war too! The *Beano*'s Lord Snooty and his pals taking on the fiendish Germans, who, dressed as Father Christmases (the swastika armbands were a bit of a give-away), deliver an unwanted gift from 'Santa Hitler'. (*Lord Snooty* © *D.C. Thompson & Co. Ltd*)

There would be no more bananas until after the war, while no lemons and no fresh or tinned fruit would be imported, except for a few oranges, because all available shipping space was badly needed for war materials. The threat of belt-tightening proved only too true: the meat ration would be cut again on 6 January to 1s 6d, and this now included cheaper meat such as offal, which had previously been 'off ration'. People had hardly started to complain when a week later it was again cut, this time to 1s 2d.

Prices were high but there was still lots of food available, and wines and spirits were plentiful. The fall of France, of course, meant that French goods, such as brandy, had almost completely disappeared from the shelves. It was reported that 'Many of the other foods and drinks you have had in previous years are dear or almost unobtainable.' Cheese was one of the latter. For other items supplies were patchy; in some areas meat was plentiful, in others not. Chicken cost up to 3s 3d per lb, and supply was short; there were plenty of turkeys on the wholesale market but they were so expensive that few shops were buying them. Pork was scarce but beef was available, although it was 'not possible to select joints'. Ham, too, was unavailable, but there was a good supply of geese costing from 1s to 2s 3d per lb, while pheasants cost 15s to 19s a brace. (Remember, the weekly meat ration was 1s 10d per person.)

In terms of fruit and nuts, all foreign fruit, such as pineapples and bananas, was extremely expensive. Oranges were in fair supply at 5½d per lb, while apples varied in price from 4d to 6d each for orange pippins. There were 'practically no' dates, figs or raisins, and grapes were very expensive, muscatels costing from 8s to 15s per lb and black grapes 3s 6d to 7s 6d per lb. Despite the official announcement that there would be 'no shortage of nuts' that year, they were expensive, with filberts and monkey nuts being cheapest at 2s per lb, with almonds at 2s 6d, brazils and barcelonas 3s, and walnuts 3s 6d, although the latter were described as difficult to find. Of the home-grown nuts, it was reported that consumption of chestnuts had 'risen in the blackout, due it is thought, to more people staying at home by their fires'. French mistletoe, another traditional seasonal product, was unavailable but people were reassured that there was plenty of the home-grown variety.

There were other shortages. Dorothy Adcock wrote:

Christmas Day loomed but there was little festive atmosphere. Being quite poor, as were most of the local people, we weren't used to anything lavish, but this year was worse than usual. However, we went to the newsagent-cum-sweetshop and asked hopefully if he had any chocolate. This had not yet gone on ration but was very scarce. He surprised us with a whole box of chocolate peppermint creams. For some reason they were in 4¼lb boxes. This, with a few balloons, made Christmas.

Official advice included: 'Overcome the sweet problem with jellies made in individual cups . . . add a slice of orange, a chunk of pineapple or a cherry to the jelly before it sets, to add colour.'

Silver coins were a traditional addition to the Christmas pudding. Silver sixpences might be used, but the smaller, round, silver 'threepenny-bits' were far better for the job. Since 1937 twelve-sided nickel-brass threepenny coins had been minted, and once again this year the Royal Mint felt the need to issue a warning that they were 'not suitable for boiling in the pudding', as had been the custom with the old silver version.

The changes which the war had brought about were reflected in the Christmas celebrations. *Woman and Home* magazine reported:

CHRISTMAS INVASION PROSPECTS.
" Now all you have to say is—' A Happy Christmas '—and you'll be all right."

In a similar vein to the Beano cartoon, Moon in the *Sunday Dispatch* shows Hitler leading his storm troopers in a cunning plan to invade Britain by stealth.

Christmas, this year, will for most of us perhaps have a deeper significance than ever before. . . . The merrymaking, I hope, will be there; the holly and the mistletoe, the opening of little parcels, the coloured paper-caps which will go amusingly well with the unusual uniforms which many of us – women as well as men – may be wearing; and although the table may not groan so heavily as at other Christmases under the burden of the good things on it, we may even get fun out of making the little less go a longer way – a sort of defiant good-humour and incorrigible happiness.

The *Sunday Dispatch* wished its readers 'Not a Merry Christmas but a Happy Christmas – Devoted to the Service of Our Country'. Sadly, the

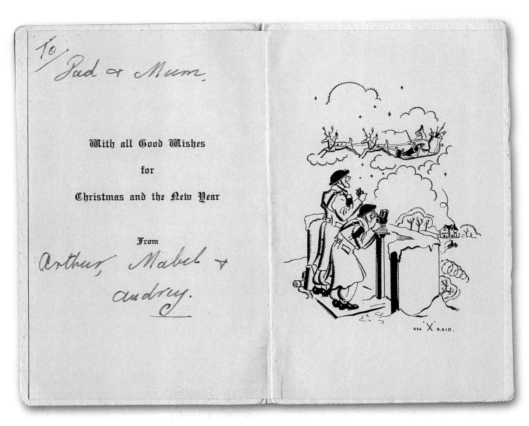

To Dad & Mum,

With all Good Wishes

for

Christmas and the New Year

From

Arthur, Mabel & Audrey.

AN X RAID.

A welcome visitor overhead from an anti-aircraft Christmas card. At this time many service groups, including the ARP and AFS, produced their own Christmas cards.

effect of this worthy front-page message was somewhat diluted by its being placed next to a large advert proclaiming 'It's a good thing to get in some Guinness'. Inside, the paper's comments included the following rousing messages: 'The less merry our Christmas this year, the more secure our chance of a victorious and merry Christmas next year', 'One bullet moulded in the munitions works is worth more to our friends than 20 greetings cards we may send to them', 'One extra bomb supplied to our airmen is better than a hundred party crackers exploded here'.

The bombing of the cities had continued throughout December and showed no sign of abating for Christmas. Few doubted that the bombing would go on over the Christmas period. In the week after the holiday *The Times* reported:

> Many people, particularly in London and the bigger towns, imported their Christmas merrymaking into the shelters. That was perhaps, above all others, the distinguishing mark of Christmas 1940. . . . The regular shelterers in the London Tube stations entertained themselves in family parties that often overlapped and intermingled. Hospitality was exchanged between the groups. Girls in party frocks whirled on the platform to dance music. In one station presents were distributed to the children from a great Christmas tree. But on the evening of Christmas Day the stations were less crowded than usual; the continuing quiet overhead had tempted some habitual shelterers to risk one night at home. The Salvation Army sent out parties of carol singers to tour Tube stations on Christmas night, handing out sweets to the children by the way and converging on King's Cross station for the final concert.

Stephen Spender wrote of 'the spirit of the Tube shelterers who went underground on Christmas evening wearing paper caps, armed against the terror of possible air-raids with Christmas crackers'. Jackie Burns was five years old at the time. 'We had a wooden indoor air-raid shelter at home, and during December 1940, because of the numerous air-raid warnings at night, my sister and I slept in the shelter. I can remember being in the shelter on Christmas Eve and seeing my father carrying a pillowcase full of presents in, sometime during the night. I think it was after that I started to wonder if there really was a Father Christmas!'

The women's magazines responded magnificently to the situation as their recipe writers came up with ideas for 'shelter-snacks': 'You will be taking sandwiches to your shelter over Christmas.' Suggestions included cream cheese spread over with redcurrant jelly; sliced tongue with watercress and a dash of mayonnaise; peanut butter with a savoury sauce, or 'two-layer sandwiches . . . Layer the first slice with galantine, cold

The lady standing beside the Christmas tree in this Ministry of Information picture is a London Transport employee selling 'Tube Snacks'; the vendors arrived by tube and dispensed hot drinks and sandwiches to the shelterers. (Crown Copyright)

meat or cold ham, spread the top of the second slice with meat or vegetable extract, and top it with the third slice. Canned tomatoes make an appetising first layer to a sandwich with a Vitamin B vegetable extract spread over the second layer.' Stork margarine also recommended sandwich fillings for Christmas, including 'sardine cream', banana and marmalade, and almonds and raisins.

Other shelter-snack suggestions included coconut cookies, 'which will not use up your rationed foods for the biscuit tin in your shelter'. The recipe used 1 cup of sweetened condensed milk, ½lb of shredded coconut and ½tsp of vanilla essence. All was mixed together until stiff, then shaped into flat rounds or pyramids on a greased baking pan, and baked in a moderate oven for 15 minutes. As a final touch they could be topped with 'glacé cherries if you've children coming to tea or sharing your shelter'. In addition 'coconut candies can be handed round to everyone'. These were made from 2tsp of unsweetened chocolate powder, ½ cup each of sweetened condensed milk and shredded coconut, ¼ of a cup of sugar, ⅛ of a cup of water, and ¼tsp of vanilla essence. 'Mix the chocolate and condensed milk, and beat in double boiler. Heat sugar and water until sugar is dissolved, then boil for one minute. Add the two together, add coconut and vanilla, arrange on greaseproof paper or pan and leave until firm.'

Not everyone took to the shelters for their Christmas dinner that year

An advert from *Woman & Home* showing how rationing was already affecting the provision of such Christmas standards as the pudding. Recipe writers and commercial suppliers would spend the rest of the war wrestling with the problem as more and more items went 'on the ration'.

For Christmas dinner this year, have a Mrs. Peek's Christmas Pudding. Saves time and money. Five other delicious varieties too. Light Fruit, Dark Fruit, Date, Ginger, Sultana.
All Mrs. Peek's Puddings are perfectly sweet. No extra sugar needed.

Mrs Peek's **PUDDINGS**

Made by
PEEK FREAN & CO. LTD.   •   MAKERS OF FAMOUS BISCUITS

but the shortages and rationing certainly affected most people's tables. The Stork margarine cookery service announced various 'savoury Christmas dishes, even in wartime . . . Turkeys and chickens may not be plentiful, so here are two mock-turkey dishes for Christmas dinner. The savoury stew can be cooked even if fuel difficulties make roasting impossible.' Chief among these 'fuel difficulties', of course, was the disruption of gas and electricity supplies by bombing. The main ingredient of mock-turkey was one rabbit, and it served four people.

MOCK TURKEY

To make the stuffing cut one rasher of fat bacon into small pieces (removing the rind). Peel and chop two onions and one mushroom, and finely chop one teaspoonful each of mint, sage and parsley. Fry bacon, add half an ounce of margarine, the onions, mushroom, and two ounces of bread crumbs, cook together, stirring well. Add a half a cupful of milk, and boil for a few minutes. Season with salt, pepper and nutmeg, and the chopped herbs and a half teaspoonful of grated lemon rind and mix well. Now wash the (prepared) rabbit in salted water, dry, and coat with seasoned flour made from two teaspoonfuls of flour, and half a teaspoonful each of salt and pepper. Then stuff the rabbit with the stuffing, melt dripping or cooking fat and baste the rabbit well, then roast in a moderate oven (Regulo Mark 4) for two hours, basting frequently.

BRUSSELS SPROUTS AND CHESTNUTS

2lb brussels sprouts
1lb chestnuts
salt and pepper

Slit shells of chestnuts and boil for five minutes. Remove shells and skin, and boil in salted water for half an hour. Boil Brussels sprouts for fifteen minutes, drain and mix with chestnuts.

Not to be outdone, *Good Housekeeping* magazine suggested the following recipe:

SHELTER CHRISTMAS CAKE

The Anderson shelter is a byword with most of us now and makes an amusing and topical subject for a cake, especially if there are children in the family.

Bake the cake mixture in an oblong mould or small bread tin and allow to cool, then cover each side with a layer of marzipan, cutting a small 'door' out of the front piece. Next, cut and fix a piece right over the top, marking corrugations with a skewer. Gather the trimmings and knead in enough cocoa to make the colour of earth, and bank them up against the sides of the shelter. Finally, cover with a layer of snow made by melting 6 or 8 white marshmallows and pouring over. Leave a clearing in front of the 'shelter' for a path and sprinkle with finely chopped burnt almonds to imitate gravel.

An Anderson shelter Christmas cake, from the *Good Housekeeping* magazine. Even the raids and the misery of nights in a damp shelter could have their funny sides. (Courtesy of *Good Housekeeping* magazine)

FOOD

Christmas Party

Quiz?

Get out your pencils, all you housewives and fighters on the Kitchen Front — and see how many answers to the quiz you get right. Top marking is 20. That would make you a cook-General! A score of 15 or over qualifies you as an Officer. If you score between 15 and 10 you won't lose your stripes, but you don't qualify for a commission. If you score under 10 you are R.T.U. (" returned to Unit ") because that must mean that you haven't studied " Food Facts," regularly appearing in this paper. *Slope Pencils! Write!*

(1) Three of the following are protective foods, three supply energy. Which is which? Carrots, flour, tomatoes, wholemeal bread, dripping, rice. (*Six marks, one for each correct answer.*)

(2) What is the principal reason why you should buy home produced foods? (*One mark.*)

(3) What is the rationed food that has recently been reduced in price, and by how much? (*Two marks.*)

(4) The new rationing period starts on one of these dates. Which is correct? January 1st. January 6th. January 15th. April 1st. (*Two marks.*)

(5) What time is the Kitchen Front broadcast? (*One mark.*)

(6) Auntie threw her rinds away. To the lock-up she was taken. There she is and there she'll stay

. . . .
Fill in the last line. (*Two marks.*)

(7) Mrs. Bardell, in Dickens' Pickwick Papers, ate " pettitoes ". What were they? (*Two marks.*)

(8) Which are the two most valuable root vegetables? (*Two marks, one for each.*)

(9) For which important cereal is Scotland famous? (*One mark.*)

(10) What is a hay-box? Is it (a) a fixture in a stable, (b) an actor's make-up box, (c) a fuel economiser, (d) a talkative old lady. (*One mark.*)

Answers

(*These are printed upside down so that you do not look before you should!*)

(1) Flour, dripping, and rice are energy foods. Carrots, tomatoes, and wholemeal bread are protective. (2) To save shipping. (3) Sugar, 1d per lb. (4) January 6th. (5) 8.15 a.m. (6) " Till the terms to save her bacon." (7) Not potatoes, as so many people imagine, but pigs' trotters. (8) The potato and carrot. (9) Oatmeal. (10) (c).

THE MINISTRY OF FOOD, LONDON, S.W.1

With the advent of rationing and shortages, the Ministry of Food introduced the 'Food Facts' bulletins which advised the public how to make the most of what they had. For Christmas 1940 it produced this party quiz.

The *Sunday Dispatch* was more concerned with what people were going to drink, and on 22 December 1940 came up with the list shown opposite.

Buying presents became more difficult – consumer goods became scarcer as factories increasingly went over to war work. Shortages of raw materials also played a part. Paul Fincham recalled that 'Christmas cards were smaller, and printed on flimsy paper. Wrapping paper and labels were harder to find.' In fact, the most popular gift that year was soap. Otherwise the emphasis was on useful presents, such as sleeping bags or Thermos flasks for the air-raid shelter. Other shelter-related gifts included camp beds and roll-up mattresses. Available from Harrods, these were 'designed for shelter use, but will also be invaluable for putting up an additional visitor during the Christmas holidays'. Jones & Higgins' advertisements proclaimed that 'Cold-weather shelter comforts make excellent gifts!', and went on to offer all-wool rugs for 21s each, and a 'two-tier metal folding shelter bed'. Other gifts with cold shelters in mind included warm dressing gowns, wool-lined bootees and slippers and of course,

CHRISTMAS DRINKS

Shandy Gaff: equal measures of ginger beer and pale ale, served ice cold.

Cider Cup: 1 bottle cider, 1 bottle soda water, 4 thin slices of orange, 2 three-inch slices of cucumber peel and 2 slices of orange peel, quarter gill of curacao or maraschino.

Hot rum punch: Dissolve 2 teaspoonfuls sugar in a little boiling water. Add 1 gill of rum, 1 teaspoonful cinnamon, and a nut of margarine. Fill up the tumbler with boiling water. Stir and serve.

Fruit Cup: can be made with the juice of 2 oranges, 1 lemon, the juice of 1 grapefruit; fill up with dry ginger ale or lemonade. Decorate with maraschino cherries, orange and cucumber peel and grapefruit slices; sweeten to taste.

Tomato juice cocktail: best made with 3 cupfuls of canned tomatoes (strained), the grated rind of 1 lemon, the juice of 1 lemon, 1 teaspoonful ketchup, half a teaspoonful of salt and 3 teaspoonfuls sugar. Mix all ingredients and chill. Shake before serving. This serves six. A few drops of walnut vinegar can be added for piquant flavouring.

Air Force: two-thirds gin, one-third lemon juice. Add 3 dashes maraschino.

Artillery: two-thirds gin, one-third vermouth or Branca.

Bulldog: Wineglass of gin, juice of 1 orange, pour both into tumbler and fill up with ginger ale. Add ice or cool before serving.

Guardsman: two-thirds gin, one-third vermouth. Add a dash of curacao.

Royal Navy: two-thirds Jamaica rum, one-third lime juice. Sweeten with sugar to taste.

'If you want to cure a Christmas chill, try warming half a pint of beer in a saucepan and adding a pinch of ground ginger; or take half pint of claret, 2 lumps of sugar, 1 slice of lemon, or 1 slice of cinnamon. Boil and sip very hot.'

At least the Christmas cheer could still be got – if not the spirits. Beer was generally available, if not in large amounts, but other beverages were in short supply.

siren suits – 'the very thing for times like these – warm and cosy'. Winston Churchill, a great fan of the siren suit, even presented the King with one that Christmas.

Woman and Home magazine's Christmas special was 'packed tight with inexpensive gift ideas'. These included, 'For that Someone who is always in search of a pencil! A whole bunch of them; indelible, soft and hard lead, two for the telephone-pad and two for pocket-books – and a scribbling block.' Or, 'For the scrap album collector – a small paste-pot transformed with green and pink paint, with a ribbon tie-up.' Or, 'Shoulder-strap lengths of pink and blue ribbon all ready to sew on with matching sewing-silk and needles – would be delightful!', and 'Is she always in search of a lost thimble? Then give her a tiny bagful – white, pink, and blue – then she will remember them most gratefully, at least once a day!'

The magazine also included instructions for making many homemade gifts, such as knitted jumpers and cardigans, and a tea-cosy shaped like a lady in crinolines. There were also several ideas for what we might today think of as 'Blue Peter'-type gifts (although there was no sticky-backed plastic in those days); these included 'a basket for her baby doll', made from a fruit punnet covered

Siren suits, either homemade or shop bought, were among a whole raft of 'shelter goods' which proved to be popular gifts that year.

People were discouraged from wasting money which should be given to the war effort, as the message of this advert from the *Kent Messenger* sums up very neatly.

in material, bordered with a muslin frill, and 'a miniature book-case for buttons and pins', made from six empty match-boxes and some pieces of cardboard.

Again, some presents were very much of the period. John Bird remembered: 'I received a rather basic homemade wooden model of the destroyer HMS *Cossack*; I believe my mother had it made by one of her police colleagues. *Cossack* was the ship which attacked the German prison

A signal success at Christmastide

'Player's Please'—that's the most popular message everywhere; particularly so at Christmastide and on all those occasions when a smoker's present has to be considered. By choosing Player's you can rest content that your gifts will always prove signal successes.

★
In the National Interest empty your packet at time of purchase and leave with your tobacconist.

Player's Please

PLAYER'S NAVY CUT CIGARETTES · MEDIUM OR MILD · PLAIN OR CORK-TIPS
N.C.C.543A

Cigarettes, while in short supply, could still be obtained, and were popular presents, especially for those in the services – some firms delivered them directly to military units and even to British PoWs.

ship *Altmark* in neutral waters [in February 1940]. The ship was full of British captives from sunken merchant ships. As the British boarding parties arrived they made the famous cry "The Navy's Here, Boys".'

Unsurprisingly, the December issue of *The Artist* magazine suggested 'for all those interested in painting what finer Christmas present than some art materials?' The advertisements in the magazine were remarkably similar. Reeves stated, 'In these trying times painting is surely one of the most happy distractions from mental worries', while James Newman's advert said, 'Today painting is one of the best distractions from the troubles of our times'. Other sources suggested jigsaw puzzles: 'They soothe the nerves and banish blackout blues'. Many chose the most patriotic gift of all – a War Bond. In the week before Christmas over £9½ million worth were sold.

Food was always welcome; homemade sweets or preserves were recommended as 'most suitable. Cinnamon drops made with sugar, cinnamon and water – tied in twists of paper – make good stocking fillers.'

The Shaftesbury Society organised parties for poor children who had not been evacuated from London. They set up a fund to pay for them and donations flooded in from as far away as Iceland, including £5 from the King, and a donation from the Lord Mayor of London's Air-Raid Distress Fund. The society looked after some 5,000 children, 'many of whom were entertained in air-raid shelters. In some cases we provided the meal, in others the entertainment.'

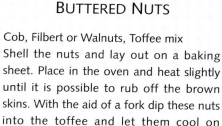

BUTTERED NUTS

Cob, Filbert or Walnuts, Toffee mix
Shell the nuts and lay out on a baking sheet. Place in the oven and heat slightly until it is possible to rub off the brown skins. With the aid of a fork dip these nuts into the toffee and let them cool on waxed paper.

Toffee mix
4oz sugar
2½ tablespoons water
½oz margarine
pinch of cream of tartar

Dissolve the sugar in the water, add the margarine and cream of tartar. Bring to the boil and cook until a little dropped in cold water turns brittle.

While many had returned during the Phoney War, many evacuees were still away from home for the second Christmas of the war. Some local authorities sent Christmas presents to their evacuees in other parts of the country. John Middleton was billeted in an evacuation hostel in the middle of Aberdare. He recalled:

Some evacuees received parcels of sweets but I did not. Only later did I find that all London evacuees received sweets from the London County Council at Christmas; we from Birmingham did not.

I was seven-and-a-half that Christmas. The postman gave me a parcel from Father Christmas. It was a box of coloured wooden strips and wheels, all with holes in, a box of panel pins, a wooden hammer, and a soft base board, about 12in by 10in, to fix the parts to. Using my imagination I could build ships, cars, even people.

Another advert urging caution and wisdom in the choice of gifts – which of course means buy their products! (*Woman & Home*)

The postman gave me another gift from himself; it was an aeroplane made from one of the old copper pennies we used then. It was beautifully crafted; no hammer or file marks to be seen.

In June, as France fell, evacuees had arrived in Britain from the Channel Islands. Many of them were children whose parents had stayed behind and were now living under German occupation. A number of them were sent to Bury, and that year John Fletcher, a retired commercial traveller from the town, started a fund to provide Christmas presents for all the Channel Islands' children between the ages of three and fourteen. He collected donations from as far afield as Canada, the USA, Australia and New Zealand and it was so successful that every child received a present worth at least 5s – a fairly large sum then.

Other people were away from home for other reasons. Eric Stevens and his family, for instance, had been bombed out during the November Blitz on Coventry:

We had moved into digs on the outskirts of Coventry but at Christmas we moved into one of my Grandad's dilapidated houses; two-up, two-down, with outside toilet. There was very little coal for heating and no lighting so we had to use candles. I can still see my mother plucking the chicken in a tin bath by candlelight.

When I woke up on Christmas morning in my stocking was an apple, some nuts and a Dinky car, but I didn't feel at all deprived.

In those days there were many childhood illnesses that were treated by sending the patient to an isolation ward. W.J. Wheatley spent that second wartime Christmas in hospital. 'I developed diphtheria and was admitted to the Fever Hospital on 6 December 1940 and remained there until 15 January 1941 . . . I was in an incubation cubicle and could only see my father through the ward window. He left a parcel for me containing sweets, comics and books with the nurses. I cannot remember much Christmas atmosphere, I was pretty fed up and spent hours reading. We celebrated Christmas on my return in the middle of January.'

There were, of course, many others away from home. By now there were almost 3 million men in the armed services; over the course of the year 41,000 of them had fallen into the hands of the enemy and were spending a bleak Christmas 'in the bag'. Many others were stationed in camps throughout Britain, and the government appealed to people with large houses to issue invitations to members of the forces to spend Christmas with them. There were also 65,000 women in the auxiliary services. The *Kentish Mercury* reported that the residents of Greenwich Borough Council's hostel for 'grass widowers – mainly munitions workers whose families have been evacuated' were to hold a party for twenty girls of a local unit of the Auxiliary Territorial Service: 'The dining room will be turned into a dance hall. This week the lonely husbands have been decorating it, and are ordering turkeys, Christmas pudding and cake. Music will be provided by a gramophone, a radio set, and other entertainments will include darts, cards and games.'

Some people had no home at all, including the many families who had been bombed out. The *Radio Times* suggested:

One way in which we can all help immediately is by making Christmas as happy as possible for the many homeless ones in our midst in various parts of the country. Give what you can in time, goods, or even money. These visitors may not all want to be entertained en masse. There are many who long for the quiet intimacy of a fireside evening. Try to discover who these may be, and give them their wish. In the bombed areas there will be lonely ones, too, whose families are far away. They would surely welcome an invitation to share the Christmas fireside of others – even if this is in a dugout or basement.

Meanwhile *The Scouter* suggested 'a good turn for Christmas', telling its readers that, 'Many boys come home from boarding schools during the Christmas vacation, strangers in their own home town. Among them are deaf boys and blind boys – some of whom are Cubs and Scouts at their schools. Of course, their parents will want to see something of them during the brief holiday but all would appreciate a visit from a Scout or Scouter.'

Lt Col Moore-Brabazon, the Minister of Transport, addressed a Christmas message to the British public. It was published in the newspapers during the week before Christmas, and part of it read:

I wish I could be a Santa Claus this Christmas and produce out of the bag hundreds of extra trains, miles of additional track and thousands of extra railway workers, so that you could travel where and as you wish – and in comfort.

Indeed, I have to curtail Christmas passenger trains and try to persuade you not to travel at all.

You know this must be a stern Christmas-tide – one during which we must work for victory. The enemy won't wait while we take a Christmas holiday, and therefore railways must continue to devote all their energies to vital war transport.

No extra holidays for railway workers – for you no extra travelling facilities. Forgive no presents this year, but best wishes for Christmas and the New Year.

Despite this appeal, on the Saturday before Christmas the stations were reported to be crowded: 'platforms seethed with people . . . most of the travellers were women. . . . At Euston hundreds of people were queuing up before 9am to get on to the platform for trains going north.'

The Post Office also made an appeal to the public, this time to post early.

Postings should be completed by December 18th, and the earlier the better . . . In normal times the Post Office has a difficult task in disposing of the heavy Christmas traffic, and the task can only be accomplished by engaging some 80,000 temporary workers throughout the country. This year the difficulties have been increased because of the release of 40,000 trained men for the Forces, the slowing up of road and rail transport by the blackout, and the need for confining deliveries, and collections, as far as possible, to the short hours of daylight.

To give some idea of the 'difficult task' which faced the Post Office, some 5 million letters were posted on the 18th alone, while ½ million bags of parcels and 25 million letters passed through the London Rail depots in the week following the 16th.

Like much else, decorations became do-it-yourself affairs. *Woman and Home* magazine's Christmas Special advised: 'Make the Christmas table special by decorating the drinking glasses with coloured stars. Cut them

Radio Times, December 20, 1940 Vol. 69 No. 899 Registered at the G.P.O. as a Newspaper

PRICE TWOPENCE

PROGRAMMES FOR
December 22 — 28

RADIO ✸ TIMES
JOURNAL OF THE BRITISH BROADCASTING CORPORATION
{INCORPORATING WORLD-RADIO}

Here is the **Christmas News** *and this is Father Christmas reading it . . . .*

'Christmas Under Fire'
Radio tour of the Empire in the front line (page 20)

'From Across the Atlantic'
Broadcasts from Canada (page 13), dance band exchange (page 21), and Hollywood greetings (page 23)

Evacuee Children
Sending greetings to their parents in three programmes (pages 20 and 23)

Pantomimes
Tour of three Northern pantos (page 16), 'The Forty Thieves' and 'The Sleeping Beauty' (page 22), 'Aladdin' (page 26)

Stars of the Week
Edith Evans,, John Gielgud, and Peggy Ashcroft (page 11), Eva Turner (page 12), John McCormack, Arthur Askey, Richard Murdoch, Elsie and Doris Waters, and Jack Warner (page 21), Sir Harry Lauder (page 30)

Music
Handel's 'Messiah' (page 11)
Bach's Christmas Oratorio (page 15)
Rutland Boughton's 'Bethlehem' (page 18)

A very topical drawing on the cover of the *Radio Times'* Christmas issue. 'Here is the news, and this is . . . reading it', was a format introduced in the late summer of 1940 to overcome the threat of bogus German stations pretending to be the BBC and giving false information. (*Courtesy of the Radio Times*)

out from gold and silver, red, green and blue paper and paste them outside the glass. Keep them all at least three-quarters of an inch from the rim.' It also suggested that pine-cone clusters should be hung about the house. These consisted of plaited strands of coloured raffia, to which were attached (with more raffia) pine cones painted 'in gay colours, gold and silver'.

The *Radio Times* suggested: 'In the centre of your Christmas table place a bowl containing holly, or a small Christmas tree, planted in earth that is covered over thickly with salt. It will look just like snow. By the same token, red candles "planted" in red bowls containing salt-covered earth give a festive air to the room, and their soft light will not interfere with your blackout.'

The Ministry of Information short film *Christmas under Fire* looked at Britain that December: 'It's not a very large Christmas tree. There's no demand in England for large trees this year. They would not fit into the shelters or into the basements and cellars with their low ceilings. This year England celebrates Christmas underground.' Although the first Trafalgar Square Christmas tree was not presented to the British people by Norway until 1947, in 1940 a group of Norwegian commandos brought a Christmas tree to London from occupied Norway for their exiled king, Haakon VII. It was a symbolic act which would be repeated every Christmas throughout the war, and eventually evolved into the present arrangement.

The *Radio Times* that Christmas wrote: 'At this time of the year, all we are usually thinking about is Christmas plans. This is the second wartime Christmas, so far as radio programmes are concerned, and the programme departments have very ambitious plans. Many of the traditional Christmas broadcasts are to be carried out, and there are many more projects that would never have been hatched but for the war.' There was now a choice of two BBC channels, the Forces Service having joined the Home Service earlier in the year. This allowed for more specific regional broadcasting, and special programmes for the Free Forces of our occupied allies, many of whom were now stationed in Britain.

Home Service programmes that Christmas Day began as usual at 7.00 p.m. with the news. The programmes contained the normal Christmas fare: carols, classical music played by the BBC and other orchestras, a Christmas morning service, a quiz, and light music shows, such as *Sandy Macpherson at the Organ*. It also included *A Merry Christmas Children Everywhere*, which consisted of Uncle Mac's Christmas carols, *The Kitchen Front* by Gert and Daisy, and *From the Children*, which was 'a radio card of Christmas greetings from evacuated children in Great Britain, Canada

Sisters Ethel and Doris Waters – alias Gert and Daisy were two very popular stars of the stage and radio. That Christmas Day they were on the Home Service twice; they delivered the Kitchen Front programme in the morning and appeared in the *Christmas Star* variety programme in the evening.

and the United States'. The *Children's Hour* programme was *A Christmas Carol* by Charles Dickens, and other special audience shows included *Gwasanaeth Gosber*, a studio service in Welsh, and the news in Norwegian.

At 2.00 there was that year's Empire greetings programme, entitled *Christmas Under Fire*. Locations included 'an English Cathedral in the front line', a Home Guard observation post, merchant seamen in a north-east port, a pantomime from Scotland, a London fire station, and an underground shelter party. As before, this was followed by the King, who spoke of 'the sadness of separation' for children and other members of the family. His message ended: 'The future will be hard, but our feet are planted on the path of victory, and with the help of God we shall make our way to justice and to peace.'

The evening's programmes included, at 7.15 p.m., the *Christmas Star Variety Show* featuring Elsie and Doris Waters (Gert and Daisy), Arthur Askey and Richard Murdoch, Jack Warner, and Geraldo and his Orchestra; this was followed by *Transatlantic Rhythm*, with two British and two American bands; *The Squeaker*, a play by Edgar Wallace; and to round it all off there was Billy Cotton and his band. Close down was at 12.20 a.m.

The forces station broadcast many of the same programmes, plus others that were unique to it, including a *Grand Children's Party*, *Vocal Jazz*, sports news from Canada, the news in French and Dutch, *The Signalman* – a ghost story by Charles Dickens, and *Stars in the Shelter* – an ENSA Christmas entertainment.

This year the pantomimes were the same but the jokes were different. The *Daily Mirror* reported: 'Last Christmas Eve the pantomime comedians were polishing up their gags about ARP and a crack about a warden was always sure of a laugh. Now the laughs have turned to cheers. ARP workers and the police are doing a more than full-size job.'

Robina Hinton remembered:

My husband Reg was in panto with Jack Buchanan at the Lyceum in Sheffield. Having lost the argument as to going in for an evening's rehearsal, he emerged at day-break to find his digs had taken a direct hit and everybody in them was killed.

I was working at the Coliseum during that year. I left it too late to get myself a job in panto, so I thought I'd spend that Christmas in Manchester with my family, only to be chasing incendiary bombs with my brother-in-law who was a Warden, obeying his orders not to bother with 'that one' until last – 'They've run off to Blackpool.'

And of course there were many small pantomimes, staged by amateur dramatic societies and other local groups. Paul Fincham recorded:

'Pantomimes were a favourite way of raising money for war funds. . . . One air-raid shelter group acted the story of Cinderella, losing her gas mask instead of her slipper. Hitler appeared as the wicked fairy!' Patricia McGuire remembered: 'I was in all sorts of concerts at Christmas as I went to dancing classes; there was always a party to follow a concert – even though there was war on we still had fun.'

At the cinema there was a choice between new releases such as Alexander Corda's *The Thief of Baghdad*, Charlie Chaplin in *The Great Dictator*, Mickey Rooney and Judy Garland in *Strike up the Band*, Henry Fonda in *Frank James*, and Bette Davis and Charles Boyer in *All This and Heaven Too*. Alternatively, at the Ritz in Leicester Square *Gone with the Wind* was 'in its 46th week'! British offerings were thin on the ground, which, under the circumstances, is understandable; they included *Sailors Three*, with Tommy Trinder, Claude Hulbert and Michael Wilding.

This year the newsreels showed footage of the Russo-Finnish war, and of various troops, principally Free-Allied units in Britain, having their traditional Christmas Dinner. One showed Father Christmas walking among bombed buildings to the commentary, 'Once upon a Christmas a very good man came down the chimney. But this year he walks among the ruins of many homes, shaking his head sadly at the work of an evil being that nobody loves'. Next, to the usual jokey commentary, we see the local children mobbing him, in scenes more reminiscent of a modern popstar, as he struggles to hand out a few gifts from his sack. Eventually the poor actor, obviously much relieved, manages to get away. 'Good old Santa Claus; coo, Mum, now we can have a Christmas tree with lights on and everything – we mustn't forget the blackout though. . . . It'll be a nice Christmas.'

A popular short film being shown that Christmas was the Ministry of Information's *Christmas Under Fire*, described by its narrator, the American journalist Quentin Reynolds, as: 'The story of Christmas in

THE PERFECT MUSICAL COMEDY.

Mickey (noted world film star No. 1) and his best loved playmate in the show which will give you the real Christmas spirit!

Mickey **ROONEY** · *Judy* **GARLAND** in **STRIKE UP the BAND**

PAUL WHITEMAN and ORCHESTRA.

To-day and Xmas Day from 1.30 p.m. Weekdays, continuous from 10.0 a.m. (U)

The **EMPIRE** LEICESTER SQUARE

ONE THOUSAND AND ONE SIGHTS FROM THE THOUSAND AND ONE NIGHTS

ALEXANDER KORDA presents IN MAGIC **TECHNICOLOR** **THE THIEF OF BAGDAD** (U)

with **CONRAD VEIDT** · **SABU** · **JUNE DUPREZ**

Premiere TOMORROW at 2.45

(in aid of the British Volunteer Ambulance Corps) Prices 2/6 to 21/. All Bookable. —then (ordinary prices) till 7 p.m.

Thereafter daily from 10 a.m. (Xmas Day from 1 p.m.)

ODEON Theatre WHI.6111 LEICESTER SQ.

BOOK YOUR SEATS IN ADVANCE... for the day and the performance you desire FOUR SEPARATE PERFORMANCES DAILY at 10.15, 12.55, 3.10 and 5.45 Sundays & Xmas Day at 2¾ and 4.30

★ SPECIAL PRICES 10 15 SEP. PERFORMANCE 1,100 SEATS from 2/9 Box Office open Sundays PHONE WHI. 8681/2

PRINCE of WALES SPECIAL *Theatre* PRESENTATION United Kingdom Premiere **CHARLIE CHAPLIN** in "The **Great** Dictator"

All Reserved Seats Book in Advance!

the exciting successor to Jesse James! HENRY FONDA IN THE RETURN OF **FRANK JAMES** (A) in *technicolor* with **GENE TIERNEY JACKIE COOPER HENRY HULL** PRODUCED BY DARRYL F. ZANUCK

TODAY at 2·35 & 5·25 p.m. WEEKDAYS at 12·45, 3·50 & 6·55 p.m.

REGAL MARBLE ARCH PAD.8011

THE **GOLDEN FLEECING** with **LEW AYRES RITA JOHNSON** An M.G.M. Picture. (A)

Also— JACK LONDON'S **QUEEN OF THE YUKON** CHARLES BICKFORD, IRENE RICH (A)

Continuous daily from 10 a.m. Xmas Day & Sunday 1.30.

Tomorrow! **LONDON PAVILION**

PLAZA PICC. CIRC...WHI.8944 Open 1.15 TODAY AND XMAS DAY Weekdays (inc. Boxing Day), Cont. 1.30·7 "A **DATE WITH DESTINY**" starring **BASIL RATHBONE ELLEN DREW JOHN HOWARD** with RALPH MORGAN

Paramount's Chilling Mystery Thriller!

PARAMOUNT'S MIGHTY *Technicolor* MASTERPIECE "**1940's BEST FILM**" DLY. MAIL Gary **COOPER** · Madeleine **CARROLL** in Cecil B. DeMille's "**NORTH WEST MOUNTED POLICE**" (U)

CARLTON Theatre Haymarket. WHI.3711

TO-DAY and DAILY at 2.0 and 4.30 (inc. Xmas Day and Boxing Day). Open 1.30. "N.W.M.P." starts 2.20 & 4 50—See it from the beginning: 1/10, 3/-, 4/6, 6/6, 8/6. Seats Bookable. with PAULETTE GODDARD and Cast of Thousands

Commencing **XMAS DAY** at 1 p.m. BOXING DAY & WEEK DAYS OPENING 9·30 A.M.

WARNER THEATRE LEICESTER SQ. GER 3423

Bette **DAVIS** *Charles* **BOYER**

Jeffrey **LYNN** Barbara **O'NEIL** An ANATOLE LITVAK Production.

The Book you've Read! The Stars you Love! The Picture you'll remember!

ALL THIS, AND HEAVEN TOO (A) From the BOOK by RACHEL FIELD

Hurry! Last 3 Days "**BROTHER ORCHID**" (A)

Charles Chaplin THE **Great DICTATOR** WITH **PAULETTE GODDARD** Cert 'U'

Written, produced and directed by Charles Chaplin.

Programmes Commence 1·30, 4·10 USUAL PRICES

GAUMONT IN THE HAYMARKET **Marble Arch Pavilion**

WILL FYFFE LESLIE BANKS YVONNE ARNAUD in **Neutral Port** Cert 'U'

Directed by MARCEL VARNEL Produced by EDWARD BLACK In charge of Production MAURICE OSTRER A GAINSBOROUGH Picture

To-day at 1·30, 3·25, 5·30.

NEW GALLERY REGENT STREET

Cinema going was very popular during the war, and many families would take in a trip to the cinema over the holiday period to see one of the many new releases on offer. (*Sunday Dispatch*)

England, in the year of the Blitz, 1940 . . . This year England celebrates Christmas underground . . . It will be a Christmas of contrasts: holly and barbed wire, guns and tinsel.' The film showed pictures of Britain in the Blitz, culminating in a memorable scene of shelterers sleeping in the London Underground, with a Christmas tree set up among them, to the sound of a church choir singing 'O, come all ye faithful'.

Another short film, entitled *Post Much Earlier This Christmas*, reflected the events of the year, and showed postmen trying to deliver parcels to bombed houses, amid streets roped off with 'Danger – Unexploded Bomb' signs, thus vividly illustrating the difficulties the GPO faced in trying to deliver the mail. *Your Anderson Shelter this Winter* advertised a government leaflet of the same name, giving various tips for improving comfort in your shelter – very relevant that winter.

As with films, the most popular music that year was escapist, in contrast to the previous Christmas's more jingoistic hits. Decca Records' latest releases for Christmas included no fewer than three versions of the latest hit 'Sierra Sue', by Flanagan and Allen, Ambrose and his Orchestra, and Bebe Daniels. Another big hit of that year, 'All the Things You Are', was recorded by Adelaide Hall and Tony Martin. Other popular discs included Vera Lynn's 'I'm Spending Christmas with the Old Folks', Charlie Kunz's piano versions of various hits, and 'Danny Boy' by Arthur Tracy (nicknamed the 'Street Singer'). All these 10-inch discs cost 2s.

The *Sporting Life* of 23 December reported on a new development in football for that winter:

Another new feature, so far as League football is concerned, is that on Christmas Day fourteen clubs will play home and away fixtures, one game in the morning and the other in the afternoon. The clubs to introduce this novelty were Watford and Luton – towns less than 20 miles apart – who decided to meet at Watford in the morning, and then, after a suitable meal, take the road for a second game at Luton. . . .

The decision to play two games on Christmas Day when the geographical position of the clubs makes it possible is inspired by the necessity to make up for the serious financial loss on the season to date.

This loss was due to the restricted crowds and the limited programme of matches. The paper did point out that after playing two matches, the players were 'likely to be dog-tired and weary'. Among those who played twice, Tommy Lawton and Ken Shackleton were unusual in that they each played for two different teams that day (Lawton for Everton and Tranmere and Shackleton for Bradford Park Avenue and Bradford City). It was by now common for teams to field guest players, who did not all share the star status of players like Lawton and Shackleton; that afternoon, for example, Brighton

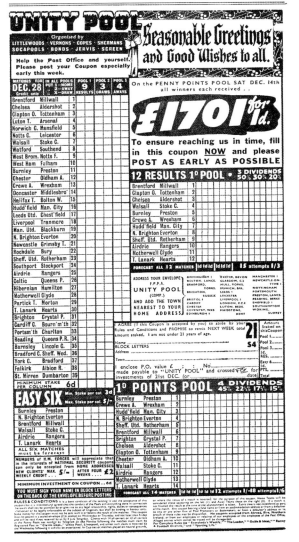

There was still a chance to dream, even in wartime you could win the football pools.

& Hove Albion could muster only five players for their away match against Norwich, so their team was supplemented by the Norwich reserves and even some supporters. Not surprisingly, Norwich won 18–0.

Attendances were up, with most crowds topping 4,000. Indeed, over 8,000 watched West Ham beat Arsenal 4–2, a crowd equalled by those at both Burnley and Blackburn, while crowds of over 5,000 saw Tottenham Hotspurs draw 3–3 with Millwall and Liverpool beat Everton 3–1.

On Boxing Day there were National Hunt meetings at Wetherby and Taunton, and several greyhound meetings, notably at Dagenham and Oxford. There were also several Rugby Union matches, including Gloucester v. Army XV and Cardiff v. Welsh Army XV.

THE CHRISTMAS RAIDS

The week leading up to Christmas saw a series of heavy raids on the industrial north-west of England, beginning on 20 December. At 6.20 p.m. that night bombs began to fall on the Merseyside area. At first it appeared to be a light raid, but from about 8 p.m. the bombing intensified and remained heavy until 11 p.m. The local fire services were overwhelmed, and reinforcements had to be called in from a wide area. *Bombers Over Merseyside*, published by the Liverpool Daily Echo and Post, described the situation:

> As always, the fire crews and rescue teams worked throughout the raid under conditions of extreme danger; one fire engine racing to an incident drove into a bomb crater, killing its crew of seven.
>
> A series of five railway arches in Bentinck Street, Liverpool, used as an unofficial shelter and crowded with people, were directly hit. This was one of the most dreadful of the night's incidents. The arches were quite destroyed, collapsing in huge concrete blocks and showers of ballast on to the packed ground beneath. The work of rescue was exceptionally difficult, since the blocks of concrete could not be moved, and were hard enough to turn the chisels of the compressors brought up to split them. After many days, when the work was complete, 48 people had been brought out alive, but 42 bodies had also been extricated.

This first raid continued until 4 a.m. the following morning. The next night, at about the same time, the first few aircraft of what was to be an even bigger attack began to drop their loads. This time the raid was in two waves – from 7 p.m. to 10.30, and then from about midnight until 3.30 a.m., finally petering out at about 5 a.m. The docks were the main target, and many warehouses were set on fire. Again *Bombers over Merseyside* described the devastation:

> Hundreds of houses were struck, especially in the Anfield district, and a single direct hit on a large shelter caused the worst single tragedy of the night. When the rescue service and the searchers had completed their work there, 74 bodies in all had been brought out for burial. The raid spread its effects over Bootle, Birkenhead, Seaforth and Wallasey, with minor incidents elsewhere, but the main burden of the blow was borne by Liverpool itself.

One feature of these raids was the extensive use of landmines. These were originally manufactured as magnetic sea mines but British boffins had found a way to counter them, thus leaving the German Navy with a large stock of redundant mines. They were subsequently converted to enable them to be dropped by parachute, as a sort of large, and very destructive, bomb. Margaret Spencer was eight years old when her life was turned upside-down by a landmine:

> Our home in Brisbane Street, Kirkdale, was destroyed by a landmine on 21st December. My mother, father, my two younger sisters and I were taken for temporary shelter to my aunt's new council house in Norris Green. This had three bedrooms but only one living/dining room. My aunt, uncle, their three-year-old son and my aunt's brother and sister were already living in the house. To make matters worse my mother was eight months' pregnant and my aunt seven-and-a-half months.

Lily Roberts remembers the raid clearly:

I was twenty years old and lived in Langrove Street; the bombing was very bad then; something fell out of the sky near us – I don't know whether it was a bomb or a landmine, but it buried a lot of my pals and neighbours and caused a large crater. We were told to go to St Polycarp's Church which was nearby. So my Mum and I and younger sister collected an elderly aunt and uncle and remained there for about four days. During this time we were cared for by the air-raid wardens. There were lots of children and old people there; we tried to sleep on the pews.

After four days we were told it was safe to go and see what was left of our homes. Then we saw the crater: half of Arkwright Street and Langrove Street had been demolished. All the windows had been blown out of our house, the doors had all been blown off, there were holes in the roof and the inside was full of soot from the chimney.

Not all the trouble was caused by explosions. Unexploded bombs caused even greater havoc, as whole streets (or, in the case of landmines, whole areas) had to be evacuated until they had been dealt with by the bomb-disposal squads. Vera Rooney wrote: 'My family lived in Othello Street, Kirkdale. On Sunday just before Christmas people in our street and the surrounding streets were told to vacate our homes because there was an unexploded landmine a few streets away. My father, mother, two brothers and I, along with many others, were put up temporarily in a room underneath Daisy Street School.'

On 22 December the *Luftwaffe* returned. This time Manchester was the main target, and the Mersey towns suffered only lightly. Just after 6.30 p.m. the sirens in Manchester, Salford and Stretford sounded. The main German bomber force had turned aside from an apparent third attack on Liverpool and was now heading in their direction. Two minutes later the first of thousands of incendiaries began to fall. Following standard *Luftwaffe* tactics, later waves of aircraft dropped increasingly large high explosive bombs into the conflagration: over 230 of them in all.

'. . . *Postman's knock—will someone just go outside . . .*'

Jack Dunkley's humorous view of Christmas in the Anderson shelter, party hats, paper chains, radio, and all, and a rather dangerous request from the announcer. (Courtesy of the *Radio Times*)

Doreen Robinson and her family lived in Salford, near the main dock gate:

We didn't have a shelter. Mum, my three sisters, my brother and me sheltered under the table. There was an unexploded bomb in our street and the ARP people came round to tell us to get out, but with all the bombing the door had jammed, and Mum had to shout to them to help us open it. At ten I was the oldest of the kids, and in the rush to get to the shelters we forgot my brother's shoes.

They sent us to St Cyprian's Church in Hodsall Lane, where we were sent downstairs. At about 5 in the morning they said we all had to move, we were too close to the fires. When we went out I thought the sky was on fire. They took us to the Central Mission on Trafford Road, about a mile and a half away; my brother was still shoeless. Next day Dad, who had been at work when the raid started, found us; they let him go back to get some clothes, and my brother's shoes, but we had to stay there for two more days.

The next night, the 23rd, the bombers came again, this time at 7.15 p.m. Les Sutton had been given Christmas leave from the Royal Welch Fusiliers, and was making his way home to Meadow Street, Ardwick. He recalled:

It was early evening of Monday, December 23rd 1940 when our small leave party bagged a carriage and soon the train was on the move, leaving behind a dark and cheerless Rhyl. . . . our chatter was of Manchester pubs and other places of mutual interest. Leave-returnees from Liverpool had recounted the air-raids on their city, but we could not know that in Manchester raids of the same magnitude had started the previous evening and that even as we travelled homewards the second big attack was on its way.

After a very slow journey the train stopped outside Warrington. We stumbled through the dark to the station platform and were told no more trains would be going to Manchester as a raid was taking place there. Not over-alarmed, we decided to hitch a lift and walked clear of the town and only then, facing home and with little to block our view, we were shocked to see the widespread glow in the east, and wondered what we were going home to. A lorry picked us up, and perched atop the load we hung on to the lashings, the icy wind whipping our faces, each of us thinking Manchester might be no more by the time we got there. The sneak raids of the past months we had heard about but this in front was quite different.

As we neared the burning city the frightening red glow reached high into the heavens and lit up the countryside. We could hear the dull impact of the bombs and the barrage set up by the big guns. As we passed through Irlam, Salford's fires could be seen plainly and in the open fields on both sides of the road scores of incendiaries were burning away. Reaching Victoria Bridge at Wooleys the lorry had to turn back because of the mass of fire hoses covering the roads like giant spaghetti – a detail I'll never forget. The firefighters, though busy and intent on their job, yet had a curious air of detachment and unconcern and from them we learned of the city's ordeal since Sunday evening.

Dorothy Adcock was among the many who had returned from evacuation to her home near Manchester:

I was ten years old by then. We lived quite close to the city on Greenheys, between Hulme and Moss Side. When the siren went we had to go down to the cellar. Mother thought the shelters were a health hazard so a bed had been placed sideways with a bench of some kind next to it to widen it. Five children including a toddler slept on it for the first part of the war. There was a fireplace in the cellar, which at one time had been a kitchen, so Mum would sit in a chair next to the fire.

Soon after the bombs started an aunt and uncle and their two sons came. The ARP warden had told them to get off the streets. They had been to the cinema. They were desperate to get home to check it was OK and decided to chance it after a couple of hours. Dad was out with the Home Guard, he came back a couple of times to check on us. He told us that he had been helping to get people out of the bombed Hulme Town Hall. Amazingly we children slept the rest of the night until the all clear.

Thousands of incendiaries and numerous high explosive bombs had been dropped in a raid which lasted until the early hours of Christmas Eve. But the rescuers' work did not stop when the raid ended. By 3.00 a.m. all the major fires were surrounded by fire appliances, but at this point a strong north-easterly wind got up, fanning the flames and scattering sparks that started new fires. Within half an hour the battle against the flames was at its height. *Red Sky over Manchester* described the extent of the blaze: 'As dawn broke the fiery furnace extended from Mosley Street across Piccadilly and beyond Portland Street. In depth, it threatened to penetrate almost as far as Princess Street.' As a five-year-old, Roy Littler had been evacuated from Manchester to Lancaster, but his parents had brought him home for Christmas: 'The night before Christmas Eve the siren went and we all went down to the Anderson. When we came out everything seemed to be on fire. My Uncle George drove a lorry – he was driving in to Manchester, he saw the fires and stopped, he was in tears – he was sure we must all be dead.'

By Christmas Day the Regional Commissioner was able to report that 'the spirit of the people remains excellent, and Manchester has been able to celebrate its Christmas'. Yet this optimistic report conceals huge sadness and loss. In Manchester alone there were 363 people dead, 455 seriously injured and over 700 treated for less serious injuries. Rescue squads had been called to 501 incidents, where they had pulled out 226 people still living and 256 dead. The fire brigades were still dealing

A canteen on the platform of St John's Wood tube station. Note the three-tier bunks, with the middle tier hooked back to provide seating. (*London Transport Museum*)

with 6 'conflagrations', 20 major fires and at least 600 smaller fires, which had completely overwhelmed the local fire brigade; some 400 appliances and over 3,400 additional firefighters had had to be brought in from outside as reinforcements. Dorothy Adcock remembered: 'There was a smell of burning everywhere and the sky had a permanent sunset appearance.'

In Salford, 276 high explosive bombs and over 10,000 incendiaries fell over the two nights, leaving 197 people dead and 177 seriously injured, while in Stretford 143 high explosive bombs and thousands of incendiaries left 106 dead and 88 badly injured. In Manchester nearly

30,000 houses were destroyed or damaged, in Salford another 8,000, in Stretford 12,000. Overall tens of thousands of people were made homeless; some found shelter with friends or relatives, yet over 7,000 spent Christmas in rest centres.

Norman Mallins wrote: 'I was eighteen in 1940, and lived in Old Trafford with my sister and five brothers. The sirens went and we all went to the Anderson shelter in our back yard. Five minutes after the sirens went our house was completely gone! The ARP found us temporary places – I joined the forces soon after, and that was the last time we all lived together.'

And along with the house went everything else. Elizabeth Toy was seventeen:

I was going on holiday in Somerset, my mother had bought me new clothes which were packed in a suitcase. My mother and sister went out while I had a bath in front of the fire. I had just finished when the sirens went; I hurriedly got dressed in a pair of slacks, a polo-neck sweater and a pair of slippers. I had just emptied the bath out of the back door when the bombs started to drop. My friend called round and we sat in the coalstore under the stairs, but as we heard the bombs getting nearer we both ran out to the shelter. When the raid was over all I had was the clothes I stood up in – our house had received a direct hit by a landmine. I had to go to Somerset in borrowed clothes and shoes – that was my Christmas present from Jerry!

As in Liverpool, unexploded bombs and landmines kept many away from home, Roy Littler's family among them.

There was a landmine at the end of our street, so they wouldn't let us back. They gave us the choice of two cinemas to go to; the King's in Regent Road (known locally as the bug hut), or the Carlton in Cross Lane. The Carlton was a bit posher, so we went there. I hoped they'd show us a film, but they didn't, so I went to sleep in the aisle. My brother Jim was in the ARP; when he got back, he stepped on my toe and woke me up. I made such a fuss, Mum didn't half tell him off! There was a chip shop opposite the Carlton, and they opened up for us, so we all had fish and chips for Christmas dinner.

They were not alone. For Doreen Robinson and the others sheltering in the Central Mission Christmas dinner was an impromptu affair, as it was for many thousands of others across Britain. She recalled: 'On Christmas Day I remember we had soup for dinner.' Meanwhile in St Polycarp's Church Lily Roberts and the others 'were supplied with cheese sandwiches and tea for our Christmas dinner'.

Even for those still in their homes the celebrations were curtailed. In Liverpool Mrs C. Thomson's family had had a near miss:

The Germans dropped a landmine in our street demolishing several houses and killing the occupants, and leaving the rest of us without gas, electricity, water, and windows. On Christmas Day my mother cooked a turkey and roast potatoes in the coal oven, and the vegetables on the hob. We ate it all by candlelight as we had to have the windows boarded up. I remember going to church afterwards, walking to Everton Valley, Kirkdale, and surveying the devastation all around and wondering what it was all about.

Dorothy Adcock's family home had survived, but they had an unexpected guest. 'The next day was quite exciting. Dad brought home a fellow Home Guard; he wasn't allowed in his lodgings as there was an unexploded landmine nearby. Our Christmas dinner was a small piece of pork, and this had to stretch to our house guest as well.'

For others the Christmas cheer had been ruined in other ways. In Manchester, for example, 'No fewer than 23 public houses and breweries, including the Woolsack, the Falstaff, the famous Blue Boar

Children sleeping in triple-tier bunks around a Christmas tree on a tube platform. Stockings have been hung from the bunks. (*Associated Press*)

Hotel and the Ship Inn in Blue Boar Court, the Old Millgate Hotel and the Coronation Hotel in Old Shambles, were destroyed; 22 others were seriously damaged, and 132 other well-known hostelries sustained lesser damage.'

In spite of all this, Christmas did come to Merseyside and Greater Manchester that year. Mrs Elizabeth Hobson was a child in the Salford area:

The nights prior to Christmas Eve had been spent in our air-raid shelter. My brother and I, along with other children, wondered if Father Christmas would be able to find us on Christmas Eve. However, December 24th came and there was no bombing raid. We were able to spend the night in our own beds. Christmas morning brought our presents and a stocking filled with nuts, fruit, chocolate bars and inevitably a brand new penny. We went to morning service and then home to an exciting Christmas dinner. We were to have a chicken, a very special treat in those days, along with the usual vegetables. My mother always made a Christmas pudding and a cake, which were delicious. The afternoon was spent playing board-games or reading our new books before we had sandwiches for tea and the Christmas cake was cut.

Margaret Spencer recalled: 'Some of our clothes and toys were rescued from the house and yes, Father Christmas did come. My main presents were two books: *Tales of the Northern Legends* by Dorothy Belgrove and Hilda Hart, and *Alfred, Lord Tennyson's Poems and Extracts from his Stories.'*

At that time it was, of course, the done thing to dress up in your best clothes for Christmas Day. But it wasn't going to be plain sailing for Vera Rooney's family. The street they lived in had been cleared for an unexploded landmine:

All our new Christmas clothes were left at our house. My mother was determined that Hitler would not spoil our Christmas – what she was most concerned about was my older brother George, who was twelve at the time. Among the new clothes was his first suit with long trousers, which in those days was very important. So on Christmas Day she broke through the cordon to get back to our house to retrieve the new clothes. She was caught by the ARP Warden, but she told him that she was determined that George would wear his first pair of long trousers for Christmas, which he duly did.

Word had been passed to the British Government via the German Embassy in Washington that Germany was prepared to suspend bombing missions against Britain over the Christmas period as long as the RAF did the same. In fact no formal agreement was made, but neither side launched any attacks between Christmas Eve and Boxing Day. There was no public announcement of the 'truce'; the weather over the Christmas period was overcast, with occasional rain except in the south, and the lack of attacks was attributed to the weather. *The Times* reported: 'The second Christmas of the war passed almost as peacefully in Great Britain as did its forerunner. The war receded into the background. There was so little air activity anywhere that this may fairly be described as a raid-free Christmas – a blessed relief not merely for the obvious reasons but also because it granted to our airmen the rest and seasonable pleasure they deserved.'

On the 27th, however, the RAF launched a series of raids on German airfields in France, to which the *Luftwaffe* responded with a short but heavy raid on London on the 28th.

That Christmas saw the last services for some time in seven London churches, which were completely or largely destroyed in the massive German firebomb raid of 29 December. This wrecked so much of the old city that it became known as the Second Great Fire of London, and photographs of St Paul's Cathedral on that day, wreathed in smoke and flames, remain some of the most striking images of the war. The seven lost churches (now rebuilt) were the beautiful Wren creations of St Brides (the 'wedding cake' church) in Fleet Street; St Lawrence Jewry in Gresham Street, with its world-famous Grinling Gibbons carvings; St Stephen's in Coleman Street; St Vedast's in Foster Lane; St Mary Aldermanbury; Sts Anne and Agnes in Gresham Street, one of Wren's smallest churches; and St Andrew by the Wardrobe in Queen Victoria Street. The cathedral itself, with its tall Christmas tree hung with coloured lamps in the porch, was only saved from a similar fate by the ferocious defence of its own fire-watching volunteers, who climbed out on to the roof to dislodge burning incendiaries and kick them to the ground below.

Stockings for us—socks for them!

Christmas presents for Britain; news of victories in Russia and North Africa meant that Christmas 1941 would be a far more optimistic one than the last, as shown in this *Daily Mirror* cartoon.

THREE

— 1941 —

The Third Christmas

Christmas 1941 was a time of optimism; Britain was no longer alone. In June Hitler had attacked Russia, diverting the *Luftwaffe* eastward. After initial successes, the German drive towards Moscow had been halted on 6 December. On the same day Britain found herself at war with Hungary, Finland and Romania. Then on the 7th the news broke of the Japanese attack on the US fleet at Pearl Harbor, followed on the 8th by America's declaration of war on Japan. The Americans were supported by Britain, which declared war on Japan that same day. Two days later Britain was rocked by the news that Japanese aircraft had sunk the capital ships *Prince of Wales* and *Repulse*, a feat that many had believed impossible. Next day the Japanese landed in Borneo, and the following night in Hong Kong. On Christmas Day Hong Kong surrendered to the advancing Japanese, although this news was held back from the British public until after the holiday.

Four days after Pearl Harbor, on the 11th, the USA also declared war on Germany and Italy. On the 15th the Russians announced the recapture of Kalinin, as the German forces began a general withdrawal along the eastern front. On the 22nd Churchill flew to Washington for talks with our new allies, and two days later British forces retook Benghazi. Public opinion felt that there was now little doubt that we would, eventually, win, despite the set-backs inflicted by the Japanese. The papers reported that 'Seven Million Americans will march to war during the next year', and hailed the 'Recapture of three towns on the

Christmas card from the newly formed National Fire Service.

Moscow front' by the Russians. By the end of 1941 over 3¼ million British men and 200,000 women were away from home, serving in the armed forces, while the number of servicemen held as prisoners of war had risen to 95,000.

A little over 22,000 tons of bombs had been dropped on Britain during the course of 1941, and nearly 20,000 civilians had been killed, yet most of this had occurred in the first half of the year. This did not, of course, mean there were no air-raid warnings in December. Doreen Last noted in her diary every warning in her native Colchester: there were none at all for the first three weeks in December, but warnings were sounded on the

20th, 21st and 23rd. Patricia McGuire recalled one amusing incident: 'We were in the middle of having the school Christmas party when the siren went. We must have looked really funny, we were all sat there in the shelter with our gas masks on, and paper hats too.'

For many, the demands of total war meant that Christmas had become a one-day holiday; many post offices and banks were open on Boxing Day, and of course Civil Defence and Home Guard personnel were on stand-by throughout, while many munitions and other war factories worked over the holiday. The *Radio Times* told its readers: 'For the people of Britain there is no doubt about the character of this Christmas. It is a Christmas of hard work. . . . it should be made clear that a Christmas of the 1941 standard, while only a ghost of the merry Christmases that are past, is also only a hint of the many merry Christmases that are to come. . . . Christmas is a war victim, but not a total casualty.' A midnight Christmas Eve communion service at Westminster Abbey was introduced; this was to be repeated each year and soon became a wartime institution. The weather didn't help: the RAF summary for Britain on Christmas Day read 'Moderate or fresh NW and NNW winds. Mainly cloudy, occasional rain. Moderate to good visibility.'

By Christmas 1941 weekly rationed foods were 4oz bacon and/or ham, 7oz butter and/or margarine (but not more than 2oz butter), 2oz tea, 12oz sugar, 3oz cooking fats, 3oz cheese (vegetarians got 12oz, and a further special ration of ½lb cheese was given to miners and farm workers), 1lb per month jam and preserves (including mincemeat), and meat to the value of 1s 2d. Eggs were also rationed, depending on availability, but typically about three per month, or twelve for children, expectant mothers and invalids. Milk was also rationed on this basis and at this time came to about 2 pints a week, with 14 pints for children under 12 months old, 7 pints for other children and 3½ pints for adolescents. The National Wheatmeal loaf was now standard.

Getting around the regulations was becoming a national pastime. Bryan Farmer recalled:

Let's talk about XMAS FOOD

There won't be turkey on many tables this year; but the Christmas atmosphere will be there and the children's eyes will sparkle at simple treats, served gaily. From what we know of you, you'll make your Christmas catering a grand success in spite of difficulties, and we're out to help you all we can. Here are a few suggestions of general interest from letters we have sent to correspondents. A Happy Christmas to you!

I'd like a recipe for Christmas pudding without eggs.

Mix together 1 cupful of flour, 1 cupful of breadcrumbs, 1 cupful of sugar, half a cupful of suet, 1 cupful of mixed dried fruit, and, if you like, 1 teaspoonful of mixed sweet spice. Then add 1 cupful of grated potato, 1 cupful of grated raw carrot and finally 1 level teaspoonful of bicarbonate of soda dissolved in 2 tablespoonfuls of hot milk. Mix all together (no further moisture is necessary), turn into a well-greased pudding basin. Boil or steam for 4 hours.

SOME HINTS FOR CHILDREN'S PARTY FOOD, PLEASE?

Chocolate squares are popular. Melt 3 oz. margarine with two tablespoonfuls of syrup in a saucepan, mix in ⅓ lb. rolled oats and a pinch of salt. Blend well, and put in a greased, shallow baking tin, flattening the mixture smoothly. Bake for half an hour to 40 minutes in a moderate oven. Take out, and whilst still hot, grate over it a tablet of chocolate. The chocolate will melt with the heat, and can be spread evenly with a knife. Cut into squares and lift out.

Amusing little figures, cut from short-crust or biscuit dough, go down well. Roll the dough about ⅓-inch thick. "People" can be made by cutting small rounds for heads, larger for bodies, strips for arms and legs; pinch the various pieces of dough firmly together. Prick out eyes, noses, mouths, with currants. If you can draw a little or have a friend who can, make thin cardboard "patterns" of animals, lay them on the dough and cut round with a small sharp knife.

Chocolate coating for your Christmas cake. Mix together 3 tablespoonfuls of sugar with 2 tablespoonfuls of cocoa and 2 tablespoonfuls of milk. Stir, in a stout saucepan, over low heat until the mixture is thick and bubbly like toffee ; then, while hot, pour it over your cake.

A Christmassy sparkle is easy to give to sprigs of holly or evergreen for use on puddings and cakes. Dip your greenery in a strong solution of Epsom salts. When dry it will be beautifully frosted.

I'll miss my gay bowl of fruit on the Christmas table. Not if you have a bowl of salad in its place. Vegetables have such jolly colours — the cheerful glow of carrot, the rich crimson of beetroot, the emerald of parsley. And for health's sake you should have a winter salad with, or for, one meal a day. Here is a suggestion; it looks as delightful as it tastes.

Salad slices. Cut a thick round of wheatmeal bread for each person and spread with margarine. Arrange a slice of tomato in the centre of each slice and, if liked, put a sardine on top. Surround with circles of chopped celery, grated raw carrot, finely chopped parsley or spinach and grated raw beetroot on the edge. Sprinkle with a little grated cheese.

Issued by The Ministry of Food.   (S25½)

1065

Had we children relied on the rations provided, we would not have had many sweets for Christmas but for my father's ingenuity. He was a railway guard, and was often in charge of trainloads of sugar leaving the sugar beet factory in our town in Norfolk. He, the driver and the fireman would shunt the loads of sugar rather roughly to ensure that some of the bags burst in transit. The sugar would then pour out of the bottom of the wagon between the wooden flooring planks and into some containers which he carefully placed there. They would then share the proceeds. But that was not the end of the story; besides gaining some much-needed sugar to boost the family's rations, he would keep some back to take to a man who lived in a caravan on the edge of town. This man had been part of a travelling fair which had been disbanded when the war started, for the duration. His job

'There won't be turkey on many tables this year' – a Ministry of Food bulletin for December 1941, giving recipes for an eggless Christmas pudding, and food for children's parties.

had been to run the rock-stall in the fair, and he still had all his rock-making equipment, so, when supplied with sufficient sugar, he would keep his hand in.

So, each Christmas, the families of a few railwaymen would have the pleasure of eating a few pounds of rock – those brightly coloured lumps of clove-flavoured rock went down a treat after the Christmas cockerel or brace of pheasants. But it was all hush hush, of course.

Clothes were now rationed, too. On 1 June Oliver Lyttelton, President of the Board of Trade, had announced that clothes rationing would be introduced the following day. Unlike food, where each person got exactly the same, clothes were rationed using a points system. Each person had a yearly allocation of 66 coupons which could be used for any items of clothing, each of which had a set points value.

By midsummer things were looking up on the food front. The first Lend-Lease agreement was passed in March and had brought the introduction of such exotic goods as Spam and Mor (sweetened ham). The arrival of Lend-Lease goods from the USA presented the British Government with a problem. Since the actual goods sent varied, as did the amounts, and delivery could not be guaranteed, the Government could never be sure that there would be enough for fair shares all round, and consequently such goods could not be rationed. It was therefore decided that a new form of food rationing would be introduced, known as points rationing. As with clothes rationing, everyone would be given a monthly allocation of points, in this case sixteen, which could be used for the various goods covered by the points system. One month's points could get you, for instance, 1lb of luncheon meat or 1½lb of canned salmon. 'Points Day' had originally been planned for 15 November, but had to be delayed owing to a shortage of points goods in the shops, so 1 December became 'Points Day'.

For Christmas the government gave 'a special ration of block suet for making puddings'. This was described by *Woman* magazine as:

Of course you would like more

CHIVERS JELLIES

but-

don't blame your grocer if they are not so plentiful nowadays. He does his best to ration out supplies when they are available.

THIS RECIPE WILL MAKE YOUR CHIVERS JELLY GO FURTHER:—
Make up *half* a pint of Chivers Jelly in usual way, then make a half-pint of custard sauce *without* sugar. When jelly is lukewarm, set small quantity in bottom of individual glasses or moulds and mix remainder with the custard. When jelly layers are firm fill up glasses with the mixture and leave to set. The above recipe provides sufficient for seven portions.

All pure fat, so you can use a little less than usual. Allow half an ounce less in every two ounces . . . and keep it in a cool place because it has a low melting-point. To shred it, use a coarse grater and have a plate of flour beside you. Flour the grater and dip the suet in the flour frequently, as you shred it. When you're making a crust for boiled puddings or for baked meat pies, first crumble the suet and crumb it in the usual way with the flour. You can get this suet from your grocer – not from your butcher.

'There can be no fat Christmas number this year. Unable to offer anything in the way of extra pages, this journal must be content to mark the season by trying to offer something a little different,' the *Radio Times* for 19 December told its readers. It went on:

No need to stress the obvious fact that Christmas 1941 will be, in a material sense, only a shadow of the Christmases most of us have known. The family table will not groan as of old under a weight of good fare. There will be vacant chairs at the table, more poignantly vacant on

Shortages of various unrationed items of Christmas fare had become the norm, and, housewives needed to use their ingenuity to provide a few treats.

the great day of family festival than on any other day. Nevertheless it is Christmas, and none can escape it, even if there were any Scrooges still around so foolish as to wish to. Christmas 1941 may be all too different from other Christmases: it will still be different from every other day in 1941.

In the last year shipping losses had reached 4 million tons. On the 15th, in a clear sign of shortages to come, the government announced that scrap-metal collection must be quadrupled. Doreen Isom remembers the collections: 'At school, after our end of term service before Christmas, we would hear which local school won the most collections: bottles, tins, tops, bus tickets, etc. Sadly we never won.'

Shortages of food, alcohol, gifts, even of books, summed up wartime Christmases.

The armed services also required vast amounts of wood for 1,001 things, and wood was one of the first items to be 'controlled'. This, of course, meant wood shortages, which in turn meant paper shortages. A Ministry of Supply order made on 12 November laid down that 'no retailer shall provide any paper for the packing or wrapping of goods excepting foodstuffs or articles which the shopkeeper has agreed to

WHAT TO DO WITH YOUR WASTE PAPER

After the Christmas season
Collect your paper wrappings,
Your parcels, crackers, comic hats,
And other festive trappings.
You'll doubtless guess the reason:
waste paper makes munitions,
A hundred thousand tons of it
May thwart the Hun's ambitions.

Picture Post

deliver'. For the same reason there was no Christmas wrapping paper to be bought, while petrol and manpower shortages meant that shops no longer delivered, so people had to struggle about carrying all their unwrapped purchases. The *Daily Express* commented that 'unless shoppers provide themselves with kitbags or paper "carriers", all the world will know this year what they have bought for Christmas – even if the purchase, to state a highly improbable case, is a bottle of whisky.'

Make-up and beauty products were extremely scarce. An article in *Woman* magazine entitled 'How to recapture your beauty for Christmas' looked at alternatives.

> Cold weather has probably parched the skin, caused little wrinkles and roughness to appear . . . If you haven't either cold cream or skin food then get almond oil from the chemist (olive oil will do too, but is not pleasantly perfumed) and massage it well into your skin every night, patting and finger-tipping the oil right into the wrinkles and roughness of your face.
>
> Bathe your wind-reddened eyes regularly with a solution of boracic crystals dissolved in warm water or, failing that, a mild solution of common salt in warm water, and use an egg-cup for an eye bath.
>
> If your lips are rough or cracked, paint them with glycerine every night, so that they will be smooth and soft by party-time.

If you cannot get the branded kind of shampoo you like, use green soap or shredded soap from the chemist, or shave some pure soap into a glass of hot water and use the liquid when the soap has quite melted, otherwise the lumps of soap will stick in your hair . . . sprinkle a little vinegar in the final rinse; it helps to cleanse away the soap and brings out the highlights. Or if your hair is fair make your own brightening rinse from a handful of camomile flowers brought from a herbalist.

As a finishing touch put a drop of brilliantine or hair cream into the palm of each hand, and brush it lightly over your hair to burnish the curls and make all the tiny hairs stay firmly in place.

To save shipping space, messages home from servicemen and women began to be microfilmed; these were called Airgraphs. The need to post such overseas mail early is demonstrated by the date of this example – 15 November.

The Post Office reported greetings telegrams up 100 per cent on the previous year, though parcels were down. To save shipping space Christmas greetings from servicemen overseas began to be microfilmed; these were known in Britain as airgraphs (in the USA they were called V-Mail). This system continued to be used throughout the war.

The Railway Executive gave up trying to encourage people not to travel. Instead, this year's appeal was 'Lighter Luggage Please if You Must Travel. Your journey will be more comfortable if you take only a little luggage. You will help to reduce congestion and avoid delay. Take sufficient refreshments to cover your train journey.' Doreen Isom recalled the difficulties of transport: 'My grandparents and great-grandparents were not able to come although [they lived] only one and two miles away as there was no transport, so after Christmas lunch we walked to one lot and Boxing Day to the other, taking our tea with us. Then, as soon as possible afterwards, father would arrange for the one and only local taxi to bring them to ours for tea and take them back.'

Food was short, but an article in *Woman* magazine proclaimed: 'Your Christmas party can still be as gay as any pre-war feast. But instead of serving a whole meal, give your guests a choice of lots of delicious little savouries.' It went on to suggest cheese biscuits, celery rolls and homemade rabbit paste sandwiches. The cheese biscuits were made with 3oz flour, 1 tablespoon of dry mashed potato, 1½oz fat, 1oz grated cheese, salt, pepper and grated nutmeg.

CELERY ROLLS
(MAKES AROUND 8 ROLLS)

½lb shortcrust pastry
A stick of celery
salt and pepper
a little milk

Roll the pastry out very thinly and cut into pieces about four inches square. Cut the celery into pieces exactly the length of the squares of pastry and lay a piece on each. Sprinkle them with salt and pepper. Damp the edges of the pastry and roll it round the celery. Brush over the rolls with a little milk. Bake in a hot oven for ten to fifteen minutes. Serve hot or cold.
Cooking time: 10–15 minutes

Betty Quiller wrote: 'I remember that, because of rationing, it was not possible to ice the Christmas cake, so my mother made a pretty "crinoline lady", which was a doll wearing a crinoline skirt made from crépe paper. This went right over the cake and made a lovely centrepiece on the tea table. It came out each Christmas and went with us if we ever stayed with relatives for the holiday to be used to decorate their cake.'

Mr Middleton, the 'Radio Gardener', warned that 'Fruit is likely to be scarce after Christmas; a good substitute is forced rhubarb. Forcing rhubarb is a simple process. You merely dig up a root or two, plant them in boxes of soil, put another box over them, and plant them in a dark, warm corner – under the greenhouse stage is an ideal place.'

Mike Owen wrote: 'I had an uncle who worked for Kent's Best Brewery in Faversham [now Shepherd Neame's] and every year he would give my father a one-gallon stone jar of special Christmas ale. It would stand at the top of the cellar stairs to keep cool. During the morning [of Christmas Day] my father would pour himself a glass, and if I was lucky I would be given a sip. I can smell that wonderful mixture of hops and malt to this day. At the same time my father would light up a "Wills Whif" cigar, my mother always bought him a packet of five at Christmas. The smell of that cigar, and the ale, were, to me, Christmas.'

He was lucky. The *Daily Mirror* of 27 December reported:

The Christmas drink shortage gave profiteers a chance to charge what they liked. But lots of people couldn't get beer at any price. The shortage was acute in districts as far apart as West London and the west of England. Bottled beer was particularly scarce. Many people spent Christmas morning in a fruitless search for a couple of bottles to go with their dinner.

In Acton over 300 queued outside an off-licence for an hour and a half, but about half of them were disappointed. Some of them got empty bottles and lined up for draught beer.

W.J. Wheatley recalled that 'A great treat at Christmas for we youngsters were fizzy drinks. There was a local company, the Tip-top Mineral Water Company; their drinks were rather exotic. Besides lemonade were orange, lime, cherry, raspberry, and best of all, ice-cream soda. My parents weren't great drinkers, but there was usually port, or port-style wine for Christmas, and my father would drink IPA (Indian pale ale), quite daring!'

That year there were no turkeys, no gin or sherry, no chocolates, no fruit and very few toys, and those which were available were shoddy and overpriced. In Hamley's even the smallest teddy bears cost 15s 6d. Gwladys Cox wrote of Selfridges: 'the Xmas decorations very piano and of course, no fandangle, no mechanical toy façade, as they usually have'. Doreen Isom described the lack of presents by the middle years of the war. 'Our stockings hung up on Christmas Eve always had some fruit, sweets, money, and a few essentials, handkerchiefs, socks, etc.' By the end of 1941 the shortage of matches had created a great demand for petrol lighters. Various government designs, often made of plastic, were produced at the controlled price of 6s 6d each.

Of course, these shortages led to overcharging. The South-Western Price Regulation Committee issued a public warning 'to prevent cruel disappointment' about Christmas stockings which were on sale: 'A two-shilling stocking shown to the committee

'The usual guff about Sub-Section 253, Allocation of Raw Materials Order, Board of Trade ...'

The sign on the tree in this *Punch* cartoon sums it up – 'No Toys' – such 'luxury' goods, where available, were increasingly expensive, even second-hand.

contained three paper caps, a paper mask and a tiny toy – the lot worth about *2d* – and pages from an old magazine.' The *Daily Mirror* wrote 'a letter to the meanest racketeer', which read:

> I saw you in a chain store buying up the Christmas toys. I wanted a bow and arrow for my boy. It was one shilling. Before I had time to catch the assistant's eye, you swooped down and bought the lot. A nice Christmas it will be for my son. No oranges, no sweets, no bananas, no dates and no joy because the toy in his stocking won't be the one he had set his heart on. Not that you will care. You will have made a nice fat profit . . . No doubt you will enjoy your Christmas on all the things we can't get, because you can afford to buy them out of your ill-gotten gains from your black market pals.

Books were still available, though in short supply. An advertisement for Thames Bookshops declared 'Books on the Soviet Union are the Best Gifts this Xmas', and offered such titles as 'Russia's story told in pictures' for 1*s*, 'A History of the Communist Party of the Soviet Union' for 1*s* 6*d*, and 'With a Soviet unit through the Nazi lines' for 2*s* 6*d*. Not unnaturally, there was considerable interest in Britain's new allies.

John Bird remembers one unusual present: 'My mother was a police telephonist and one Christmas she knew that like all small boys I was war mad and could not get into the war quick enough. This particular wartime Christmas she managed to get me for Christmas a new hand grenade! I only threw it once in the lane where we lived, and it broke! It has puzzled me for years; are grenades not supposed to be thrown more than once? I will never know. I do know my mates envied me! Need I say it was empty of gun powder!'

The answer, for many, was to make your own presents. In the lead-up to Christmas the magazines were full of ideas. Margaret Spencer recalled:

My aunt's younger sister worked at the Royal Ordnance Factory nearby, and she got some brooches made out of pipe-cleaners and insulated wire which we used as Christmas gifts. As far as I can remember quite a bit of trading took place outside the factory gates at dinner time; Spitfires and brooches were made out of coins, etc. Papier maché fruit was painted and put in nets to hang on the tree, underwear was made from parachute silk.

Arnold Beardwell remembers two presents he received: 'One was a small steam engine (my Dad got this second-hand, and, being an engineer, did it up). The other was a wooden model of a Stirling bomber on a base, and the inside of the Stirling lit up – Dad made this himself.' Raymond Gibbons' present was even more exciting: 'My father worked at Joseph Lucas as a polisher. He made us scooters, one each, and as you could not get wheels, he made them out of old polishing mops. Five o'clock Christmas morning when we all awoke and saw our scooters, we jumped up and started pedalling them around the attic, waking everyone up with the noise of the mops!' Vera Sibley's recollections were more typical of the time:

I don't remember any presents but those we made ourselves. Knitting wool was scarce, so we

'Pre-war Christmas value for the Children' boasts one advert. Gifts were often practical, or homemade, as this advert shows.

had to undo old jumpers and wind the wool round a bottle filled with hot water; you left it to cool and you had nearly new wool. I bought some old seamen's socks for 5*s* and had lots of green wool to use; I made gloves, slippers, handbags, bedsocks and hats. People were glad of any present. We also bought, when we could get it, any old curtain material, which we washed and pressed, and used to make cushions, tea cosies, nightdress cases – all sorts of things. We also made necklaces and bracelets out of coloured buttons which looked very attractive. I once bought a piece of blue/green parachute silk for 10*s* (a lot of money in those days), and made some lovely underwear which was pure luxury.

Grace remembers: 'Old toys were repainted; my brother made one of my boys a fort, the other a garage from an old chest of drawers and paint we had left over from decorating.' Of course, not everyone was a craftsman, and their efforts were far from professional, as Margaret Spencer wrote: 'The Christmas

CHRISTMAS PARCELS

Help the Railways to keep the lines clear for War traffic by sending as few Christmas parcels as possible.

RAILWAY EXECUTIVE COMMITTEE

Every year the Railway Executive Committee issued its appeals to try to keep rail transport free for vital war supplies – without much success.

toys I most remember were a wooden doll's house and furniture which my father made. He had no idea of "scale", so we could only just about fit one chair in a room – but we loved it! My Gran bought two golliwogs stuffed with straw from a pawnshop. This caused a row because my mother thought they were un-hygienic.'

Doreen Isom recalled the part played by the Girl Guides: 'In the Guides we paid monthly visits to the local hospital on a Sunday afternoon

There were still cigars – if you could get them. If not, there was always a National Savings gift token!

to sing hymns during a brief service by our local curate. It was always arranged that the visit nearest to Christmas we would be on the children's ward to sing carols and take gifts that we had made (which went towards the Guide Needlewoman badge). Most of these gifts were toys, made out of outgrown clothes and stuffed with cut-up old stockings. Sometimes outgrown jumpers, etc., would be unravelled, then knitted into toys, etc., for the knitter's badge.'

Mike Owen clearly remembers that 'About a week before Christmas we would make paper chains by joining gummed strips of paper together to form links. If we were very lucky we might have a paper bell that opened and was hung from the centre of the room. Holly would be placed upon the top of the pictures.' Many others, such as Roy Proctor, 'made our own decorations using flour and water paste', while Margaret Spencer recalled: 'The other children and I made paper chains to decorate the room and small cardboard boxes to decorate the tree.'

Real trees had by now become very difficult to obtain, especially in the towns. In Mike Owen's family 'a very small Christmas tree would be put into a bucket of earth, which was covered in crépe paper.' Some people, like Doreen Isom, had their own tree: 'We had a Christmas tree dug up out of the garden and put back each year.' Others resorted to artificial trees; goose-feather trees, many of them made in Germany, had been popular before the war, while others were made from tinsel on a wire frame.

London Underground staff decorating a tree. Notice the prevalence of female staff, typical then as more and more men were called up. (*Hulton Getty*)

These would now be brought out annually, becoming increasingly threadbare as the war dragged on. Tree decorations were also makeshift; pipe cleaners provided a useful source of handmade decorations, shaped into stars, animals and so on.

Wendy Peters recalled: 'Christmas trees must have been in short supply, we couldn't get one, so my ingenious mother made a huge snowman frame from chicken wire, then covered the whole thing in cotton wool. I remember her having a large roll, and unrolling it in large lengths. The snowman had a face on both sides of its head so that he could be seen grinning out from the window, and inwards into our sitting room! Daddy fixed up a bulb inside, the whole thing was amazing when it was illuminated.'

The Times of 27 December commented: 'This one-day Christmas was essentially a communal festival. There were, for instance, the thousands of men and women in the Forces, and the children now living in greater safety in the country, all of whom celebrated together in large and happy families. London children in the country were not forgotten by the L.C.C. and the borough councils of Greater London who contributed £17,900 for parties and entertainments in which local children will join.'

Brenda Dudley recounted a Boxing Day visit to relatives:

After tea we played games, including Tippit. The table had a thick cloth which hung over the sides. Equal numbers of people sat each side. A thick button was secured in someone's fist after lots of fumbling under the table cloth to disguise who actually had it. Everyone then put their fists on the table. The people on the other side of the table then took turns to find out who had the button. 'John, move your left hand', 'Jack, remove your right hand' and so forth. By studying the people's facial movements or the tightening of the hand someone was asked to 'Tippit'. This was then repeated on the opposite side of the table.

Mrs Sewell recalled: 'We'd play board games like snakes and ladders.'

This year's Christmas Day Home Service schedule included: *Hello, Children*, in which Uncle Mac acted as a link for special greetings to children from different parts of the country, *The Kitchen Front*, a message to the housewife from the Minister of Food, Lord Woolton, *Workers' Playtime*, from a factory 'somewhere in Britain', and *To Absent Friends*, an empire-wide hook-up. This was promoted in uplifting terms: 'On the third Christmas Day of the war, the peoples of the British Commonwealth and their Allies are linked again by radio to send greetings to the men and women everywhere

'The toast is "Absent Friends".' An illustration from the *Radio Times* illustrating the annual Empire link-up programme, this year entitled *Absent Friends*.

fighting in the cause of freedom.' The King spoke of 'the men who have come from afar standing ready to defend the old homeland', and addressed the 'coming generation – the boys and girls of today, the men and women of tomorrow. Train yourselves in body, mind and spirit so as to be ready for whatever part you may be called to play, and for the tasks which will await you as citizens of the Empire when the war is over.'

Evening programmes included *The Striped Chest*, a short story by Sir Arthur Conan Doyle, and *Old Mother Riley's Christmas Party*, with Arthur Lucan and Kitty McShane, Billy Bennett, Dorothy Carless, Tommy Trinder and Geraldo and his Orchestra.

Forces programme alternatives included *Any Christmas Questions*, a Brains Trust special, the pantomime *Dick Whittington*, starring Will Fyffe and Harry Gordon, *ENSA Stirs the Pudding*, and a radio version of Disney's *Snow White and the Seven Dwarfs*.

Pantomimes were not the only theatrical offerings at Christmas. London's West End put on quite a selection that year: at the Apollo Edith Evans was starring in *Old Acquaintance*, at the Piccadilly there was Noel Coward's *Blythe Spirit*, at the Palladium Ben Lyon, Bebe Daniels and Tommy Trinder were starring in *Gangway*, while at the Savoy *The Man who Came to Dinner* had Robert Morley in the title role. On Christmas Eve *A Midsummer Night's Dream* opened at the Strand Theatre, with Donald Wolfit as Bottom. Robina Hinton recalls:

What happened is that only the West End shows carried on over the Christmas season – everyone else would stop the show they were doing and do a panto. So outside the West End, theatre troupes shifted over to panto for the Christmas season because people wanted families to come in. *Peter Pan* and *A Christmas Carol* were very popular. My husband and I used to be father and mother bear and employed the baby. It was a good act and we earned good money doing it.

Panto would go on for much longer than now – three weeks was a short panto but the big ones like Formby's, that ran in Birmingham until Easter. Usually they would go on for a couple of months. You had two weeks' rehearsal time.

We did not celebrate Christmas really – panto started on Boxing Day – so we used to have a pleasant Christmas but quiet. My husband and I did not drink anyway, as it would have been dangerous to do our act that way. Sometimes you would have to go in on Christmas Day to make sure everything was ready for the opening on Boxing Day. So things could be very subdued.

On the other side of the curtain Doreen Isom remembers going to the panto: 'Children's Christmas parties ceased, but the local Guides, then Sea Rangers, arranged for an alternative – an afternoon trip to the pantomime at the local repertory company.' Of course there were many amateur shows as well; the newspapers reported that 'The King and Queen had front row seats to see Princess Elizabeth as Prince Charming and Princess Margaret as Cinderella in a children's pantomime. Cinderella made the audience join in and asked her father to "Sing up and set an example"'.

As usual there was a good selection of films from the US, including Walt Disney's latest full-length cartoon, *Dumbo*. The film critic of the *Daily Express* was enraptured: 'Narkers who said Disney was slipping when he made *Fantasia* and *The Reluctant Dragon* can cease narking. *Dumbo*, his fifth full-length cartoon, is a masterpiece. . . . Children – save your pennies.' Other US offerings included Ginger Rogers in *Tom, Dick and Harry*, Cary Grant and Joan Fontaine in Alfred Hitchcock's *Suspicion* and Robert Montgomerie, Evelyn Keyes and Claude Rains in *Here comes Mr Jordan*. Even Hollywood couldn't ignore the war, and war-related films included Gary Cooper in Howard Hawke's *Sergeant York*, and Tyrone Power and Betty Grable in *A Yank in the RAF*. Those who preferred musicals could see Deanna Durbin and Charles Laughton in *It Started with Eve*, or *The Birth of the Blues* with Bing Crosby and Mary Martin.

British films included *Hi Gang!*, starring the American couple Ben Lyon and Bebe Daniels, supported by British comedy veterans Vic Oliver, Moore Marriott and Graham Moffatt. There was also *Burma Convoy*, starring Charles Bickford, a flag-waver about the drivers who carried munitions along the Burma Road to the Chinese Army, and a film version of A.J. Cronin's Victorian melodrama *Hatter's Castle* with Robert Newton, Deborah Kerr and James Mason.

This year's newsreels celebrated Britain's newest ally; one, entitled *America at War*, showed scenes from Pearl Harbor, angry American crowds outside the Japanese embassy, President Roosevelt signing the declaration of war against Japan and making his bold speech, in which he announced 'We are now in this war, we are all in it, all the way. We are going to win this war and we are going to win the peace that follows.' A second newsreel showed Churchill and Roosevelt making Christmas speeches in Washington. Churchill's speech displayed his usual love of words:

Here, in the midst of war raging and roaring over all the lands and seas, creeping nearer to our hearts and homes, here amidst all the tumult, we have tonight the peace of the spirit in each cottage home and in every generous heart. Therefore we may cast aside, for this night at least, the cares and dangers which beset us and make for the children an evening of happiness in a world of storm. Let us resolve that by our sacrifice and daring these same children shall not be robbed of their inheritance or denied their right to live in a free and decent world.

Another item showed the Queen visiting workshops to see goods made by disabled servicemen.

Government shorts included an animated film of a telegram unfolding itself out of an envelope. The message read: '[to] The British public everywhere. Many thanks your response my post early for Xmas appeal last year. I know you will do even better this Xmas. Postmaster General', while in another the comedian Max Miller appealed for salvage. Popular tunes that year often had a wistful theme, including 'When They Sound the Last All Clear', 'Ma I Miss Your Apple Pie', and 'The King is Still in London'.

On Christmas Day the usual football matches took place. Once again, attendances were up. Six thousand watched Leeds beat Huddersfield Town 2–1, while eleven thousand saw Stoke City beat Liverpool 4–3. Other matches on offer included a rather unusual local derby between Manchester United and Manchester City (drawn 2–2). What made it so unusual was that both teams were actually playing at home: United's ground, Old Trafford, had been bombed in March, and City had kindly allowed them to play their home games at Maine Road, a situation which would continue until 1949.

Bristol City were playing away at Southampton, and transport difficulties meant that the team travelled in three cars. Unfortunately,

Sheet music demonstrating the that the King – and London – are still very much alive and kicking.

Charlton Athletic v Stoke at the Valley, December 1941. Attendance at football matches, which had fallen badly at the beginning of the war, had by then risen sharply, as can be seen from the crowd. (*Empics*)

only one of the cars, containing the centre forward, a full-back and the team kit, arrived. The start of the match was delayed for a hour but the missing team members had still not arrived, so the match kicked off with Bristol's two players supplemented by five Southampton players, the Southampton trainer and three spectators. The missing cars finally arrived twenty minutes later. One had broken down en route and the other had stopped to help, but the match was played out by the scratch Bristol team. Southampton won 5–2, an honourable defeat for the Bristol team under the circumstances.

If football teams found it hard to field eleven players, Rugby Union teams found it extremely difficult to find fifteen. Most of the rugby seen at this time was either forces' teams or public schools' teams; the main match that Christmas was the Home Counties Public Schools' team against the Rest of England Public Schools, which was won by the Rest of England by 34 points to 11.

On Christmas Eve there were greyhound meetings at Harringay, Park Royal, Wembley and Cardiff, and there was another crop on the 27th. There was also horse-racing at Cheltenham and Wetherby.

CHRISTMAS IN THE COUNTRYSIDE

Setting aside the lack of air-raids, there were other major differences between urban and rural Christmases, not least in regard to the food situation. Jenny D'Eath summed it up: 'We were very lucky; because my grandparents had a mixed farm we did not have to survive purely on the rations.' Similarly Arnold Beardwell recalled: 'My sister and I, with our parents, used to visit our grandparents in Witham and Langford. As both our parents came from large families, there were house-fulls. In spite of the shortages there was plenty to eat; I remember walking along the river with my uncle to collect moorhens' eggs; big gardens full of vegetables; rabbits and chickens in abundance.'

On the other hand, in the middle years of the war many rural areas were still not connected to the basic services of water, electricity or gas. Mrs Janet Houghton clearly remembers Christmas 1941 in just such an area:

I was evacuated to Dymock in Gloucestershire in November of 1940. The family's name was Badham and all the family used to call them Mam and Dad Badham. I most remember Christmas 1941. The first thing I remember is going over the road to the woods to dig up a fir tree, which was an adventure to me. I can see us now, Dad Badham, Jean and I, pushing a barrow with a spade in it. The next memory is being in the front room of the bungalow, it is dark and the tree is sparkling. I think it was Christmas teatime because candles, which the lights must have been (there was no electricity or running water in the bungalow), would only last for a short time. The presents that I remember were a hand-knitted doll, a pair of grey knitted gloves and a Pip, Squeak and Wilfred book.

Brian Martin recalls a wartime Christmas in Suffolk:

At Ousden village primary school near Stowmarket we used to be taken on an annual visit to Felixstowe for the day in summer and at Christmas time have a bumper party; [there was a] Christmas tree with presents for everyone in the village hall.

The annual Christmas paper decorations came out every year, but in addition we would find strips of black and silver paper, used [by aircraft] for jamming radar, lying about in the fields and sometimes still tied in a bundle, and we used this for decorations as well.

Living on a farm we had eggs, milk and poultry. We bought a turkey for Christmas and pickled a pig just before it. There was a little extra fruit allowed so mother made a Christmas pudding and a cake for icing.

As we only had a Florence oil stove with an oven over the burners the cake was taken to our local bakery for a gentle bake after the bread had been baked. Just a small charge was made.

Christmas morning we would light the dining-room and drawing-room fires. Every Christmas one of our neighbours would come to dinner and tea. One thing that was never missed in our house was the King's speech at three o'clock. After that our neighbour would go home to feed his animals and we would feed ours, collect the eggs, and shut the poultry huts up when it was dark to keep the foxes out.

This would give us an appetite and we'd all sit down again for tea at about six o'clock, after changing back into our best clothes. The evening was spent chatting and having a drink in front of the wood fire.

Boxing Day we had on our own. Soon after Christmas we would have tea and spend the evening with some of our neighbours in turn, and then they would come to us. As you can imagine the evening was mostly farming talk with a drink and a smoke. I was strictly forbidden to start smoking (little did they know that when we had two Italian prisoners living with us, two of their friends on another farm were non-smokers and gave their allocation to me!) These evenings generally ended with cards for halfpenny or penny stakes just to make it more interesting. In one house I remember a bowl of large lumps of bomb-damaged chocolate that was sent for animal food.

Edith Wilson recounted one beautiful memory:

In 1944 I was fourteen years old and living on a farm in Fressington, Suffolk. My job was to feed the chickens, which I had to do every morning and evening. I went out to do this as usual on Christmas morning to find there had been a very sharp frost. The ground was white, and also the trees and hedges, which were hung with hoar-frost. The sky was a wonderful blue, with not a cloud to be seen, and across the countryside came the sound of carols being played across the tannoy at the American air base about five miles away. I shall never forget it.

" 'Good morning,' we said. 'We want to find out about your coal.' 'Cold? Aiy, that it is! Don't come up to the winter o' twenty-one, though!' "

Illustration from *Motor Cycling* magazine showing a country pub at Christmas time with locals and 'furners', in this case soldiers, probably stationed at a nearby camp. What with these and 'vacees', the traditional peace of the countryside was very much disturbed during the war.

Of course many evacuees were enjoying a country Christmas for the first time. Elizabeth Hobson was one of them:

> At the beginning of 1941 I had been evacuated and was living on a farm in the beautiful Lune valley. This was a real culture shock for a townie, in more ways than one. The family owned the farm and were gentlemen farmers; they enjoyed a standard of living far higher than that which I had been used to. I was made very welcome and I will never forget the years I lived there. As Christmas 1941 approached preparations were made which included gathering holly and mistletoe from the nearby woods. I had only seen holly and mistletoe hanging up for sale in the greengrocers' shops. Christmas morning came and all the family presents had been placed at the foot of the tallest Christmas tree in a house. As a special treat for me a stocking filled with nuts, etc., had been left in my bedroom. After morning chapel it was back home and everyone helped to prepare the Christmas dinner. I helped to set the dining table and I can remember being puzzled because I had not seen any evidence of a chicken or any roast meat but when we were all sat at the table a large dish was brought in on which rested a great goose. My face must have been a picture for I had never seen such a large bird . . . it really was something special. After dinner we got ready for a family party to be held later in the day.

The *Kentish Mercury* of 24 December ran an article called 'Christmas With The Evacuees' listing some of the activities that evacuees from south-east London were treated to. For example:

> A message referring to Woolwich, Greenwich and Surrey Docks children at Brecon says that preparations for Christmas festivities are in full swing, including 'parties, presents and pictures', with a 'big party' organised by the WVS as the highlight of the weekend.

The band of the famous Welsh Regiment will entertain the children, and at most schools Nativity plays will be presented. One of these plays will be produced in the ancient church at Llanarthney.

At Carmarthen, Woolwich, Greenwich and Camberwell children will have an interesting holiday in view. There will be a mobile cinema showing *Oh, Mr Porter*, featuring Will Hay and the ever-popular 'Mickey Mouse' films. There will be a series of parties, with Christmas trees, presents, carols and Nativity plays.

In Llanelly, where the girls from Mary Datchelor Senior School, Camberwell, had been evacuated, 'girls of the science forms are visiting the Llanelly steelworks, in the charge of Mr Glanville Williams. The special event of Christmas week will be a party for mothers and young children and an "At home" at the YMCA.'

In addition, 'Camberwell children in the Rhondda Valley Area will be provided with a full and entertaining programme of festivities. Tea parties, concerts, free cinema matinees and Christmas trees with presents for every child figure in a programme supervised by evacuated teachers and teaching staffs of the Rhondda Local Education Association.'

These special events for evacuees did not always make for friendly relations with the local children. In *William and the Evacuees*, published in 1940, Richmal Crompton's irrepressible William Brown and his friends discuss the problem:

'We want to be 'vacuated too,' said Arabella Simpkin, a red-haired, long-nosed girl, who automatically constituted herself leader of any group of which she formed part. 'They get all the fun . . .'

'Yes,' grumbled Frankie Miller, a small, stout, snub-nosed boy of seven. 'They got a Christmas party an' a Christmas tree.'

'An' tins of sweets all round,' put in Ella Poppleham, a morose-looking child with a shock of black hair and a squint. 'A whole tin of sweets each. It's not fair it isn't. Puttin' on side an' havin' parties an' eatin' whole tins of sweets. It's not fair. We oughter be 'vacuated too.'

THERE will be very few toys in the shops this Christmas, but there is no reason why you should not have plenty on the family tree, provided you are ready to spend a little time and thought on making them.

Here are several fascinating ideas which those who are quick-fingered will be able to make quite easily. As you go along other notions or variations of some of these toys will suggest themselves.

You need brightly coloured enamel paints in as many colours as you can find; glue; small pieces of stout paper or thin cardboard; and plenty of space to work in, as you are going to make a glorious mess.

First comes the Tree

Roll a tube of thick paper, any colour, like this: The ends, snipped down for 2 inches, are bent outward for the base and inward for the tip later on. Glue firmly in position along the long edge and paint any bright colour.

Now make different sized squares of paper, the largest 15 inches square, and the smallest 6 inches square. Roll these into cone shapes, glue in position, and paint green. When dry, fix to trunk like this with fine twine or linen thread. Use a sharp needle that will pass through the tube easily without bending it out of shape. Cover main trunk in this way, the small cones at the top and the large ones at the bottom, working up from the base. Paint a few white or silver spots here and there on the cones, or, if you have any silver frost, stick on some of that instead.

Finish off the top by gluing together the slits at one end very firmly so that they form a point to be gathered together at top by a big ribbon bow. This tip is *please turn to page 4*

Home Made Decorations for Christmas 1942

Angel on the Top

CUT skirt from diagram and make slit X-Y after gluing A - B. Cut heads from transfer, glue together and paint. In the original each side has slightly different colouring. Insert body at X-Y after painting skirt.

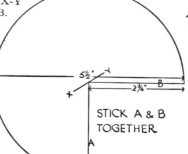

STICK A & B TOGETHER

● Shapes for the angel, horse and cart, flowers, house, lamb, and lobster, are on Transfer No. 263, price 7d. post-free in United Kingdom from STITCHCRAFT, 188 High Holborn, London, W.C.1.

motor wagon

TAKE an ordinary match box and draw out the inside for ½-inch. Paste a piece of paper round to keep inside in this position. Take a second case, if possible slightly smaller than the first, paste paper over the open ends and glue over top of first box. Make wheels ¼ inch diameter and glue in position. Paint and varnish.

3

FOUR

The Fourth Christmas

By Christmas 1942 there was a general feeling that the corner had been turned. In August the German army's advance into Russia had been held at Stalingrad. British forces were also fighting back; in late October/early November the Battle of El Alamein had been fought and won by Montgomery's courageous Desert Rats, and Rommel's vaunted *Afrika Korps* had been driven back from the very verge of victory in the Middle East. During December the Axis forces came under pressure on several fronts. The Russians launched a successful counter-offensive, British troops were advancing in Tunisia, American and Australian forces were counter-attacking in New Guinea, and day and night raids against Germany by increasingly large numbers of British and US aircraft were commonplace. Meanwhile the air assault on Britain had eased considerably; over the course of the year just over 3,000 tons of bombs had been dropped, resulting in 3,200 civilian deaths – a big drop on the previous two years.

The *Picture Post* of 26 December commented:

We can afford to think of peace for a few hours on Christmas Day, not because we are tired of war, but because we are nearer to victory . . . Think of last Christmas. Then too, we were celebrating an advance along the North African coast; our army had just taken Benghazi. But the ominous dark cloud was growing larger on the eastern horizon. After seven weeks of resistance, the garrison at Hong Kong had been forced to surrender, and we felt we were at the beginning of a long trail of catastrophe . . . That Christmas we were too near the bottom of our fortunes to show our confidence openly.

One clear sign that the country was now looking more confidently towards victory was the publication of the Beveridge Report setting out postwar social provision: 'The advent of Christmas has this year been made joyful by victories against the foe. On top of them has come the publication of the Beveridge Report, which seems like a splendid Christmas present, or Christmas box.'

The *Radio Times* was in bullish mood:

The people of Britain and her Empire, and her Allies, for the past three Christmases of this war have had little or nothing to celebrate. And it seemed as though this year there would be even less celebration. The long-awaited offensive had begun, but quietly. Mr and Mrs Smith, listening to warnings that there would be little mincemeat, few turkeys, few Christmas puddings, few toys for the children, hardly noticed its beginnings.

Then came November – and the victory of the Battle of Egypt, the landings in North Africa, the Russian attacks on several fronts, the bombings of Italy's industrial cities and harbours, the gains on sea and land in the Far East. Results at last for all the planning and training and toiling and belt-tightening! The bells were rung and the people rejoiced.

By now, 3¾ million men and 350,000 women were serving in the forces, while the number of British servicemen in enemy hands was over 100,000.

Even the weather was brighter in some areas for Christmas in 1942. The RAF weather summary for Britain on Christmas Day read: 'Light, variable wind. Mainly overcast, and much low cloud and fog in most districts. Fair and almost cloudless in South Midlands of England.' *The Times* for 28 December commented: 'The Christmas weather is still the censor's secret; it may be permissible to say that it might have been worse.'

The midnight Christmas Eve communion service at Westminster Abbey took place for the second year; *The Times* reported that 'although almost every means of transport had stopped for the night, the Abbey was packed and scores stood. There were probably more people than at the first service last Christmas Eve. The service, which lasted well over an hour, was conducted by the Dean.' In another clear sign of the government's confidence, churches were allowed to sound their bells on Christmas morning for the first time since 1939.

But life was still hard at home. British shipping losses by this time were at their height, with 7.6 million tons lost over the last year. By Christmas, weekly rationed foods were 4oz bacon and/or ham, 6oz total of butter and/or margarine (not more than 2oz butter), 2oz tea (for over 5s only, the tea ration for younger children having been abolished in July and replaced by orange juice), 8oz sugar, 2oz cooking fats, 8oz cheese (16oz special), jams and preserves 1lb per month and meat to the value of 1*s* 2*d*. Eggs were down to about two per month, or twelve for the priority groups.

In the summer, supplies of powdered egg had been made available to the public on a ration basis. A packet, equivalent to a dozen eggs, cost 1*s* 9*d*, and the ration, depending on availability, was about one packet every eight weeks (doubled for children under six). Over the Christmas period normal milk rations were about 2 pints a week. Sweet rations, introduced in July, were now fixed at 12oz a month.

The monthly allotment of points was now up to 20; with this you could, for instance, get 2½lb of imported canned fruit, or 1lb of canned boneless chicken or turkey, or ½lb each of dried prunes, figs, dates, apples and sultanas. Syrup and treacle, previously part of the preserve ration, were now on points, as were biscuits. People started to save their coupons, or items of food, for months before Christmas. With the points system shoppers were not tied to a single supplier as they were with rationed items, so they could shop around to see who had anything new in. In an attempt to prevent profiteering, on 22 December the government decreed that caterers must not raise charges over Christmas.

Welcome Always—
Keep it Handy

GRANT'S
MORELLA
CHERRY
BRANDY

P.S. Stocks still available
but restricted

Domestic soap had been rationed in February owing to the shortage of fats used in its manufacture – there was a choice of either 4oz of household soap or 2oz of toilet soap per person, per month. The basic petrol ration was completely stopped in March, and from that date only those who could prove they needed petrol for the war effort were given permits, along with professionals such as doctors. Once again, alcohol was difficult to get unless you were a regular at the pub or off-licence.

In December the Ministry of Food addressed housewives: 'Our compliments and thanks to you all. For it is thanks very largely to you for so loyally and so helpfully working with us that on this, the fourth Christmas at war, the nation's health is on a sound footing. But though "good living" must now be taken in the sense of healthy living, instead of luxury living, and we must all go carefully with fuel, we can still make Christmas fare hearty, appetising and tempting to look at.' The *Radio Times* was equally up-beat:

We're short of turkeys, short of beef, and other juicy joints,
But Christmas cheer is flowing here and you can't put that on points.

Turkeys were indeed very scarce. The government had controlled their price, leaving farmers little profit margin, and consequently very few

TWO TURKEYS

Don't make Christmas

BUT **ONE**

IN SOUP, STEW
OR VEGETABLE DISH

FOR CUP AND COOKING
OXO CUBE
MAKES PERFECT GRAVY

Makes it **BEEFY** !

'Two Turkeys don't make a Christmas' – which was just as well, as by now most people couldn't even get hold of one!

were raised commercially. People made do with what they could get. Mrs D. Wilkins recalled:

One of our neighbours, a river policeman, gave us some pigeons that had been trapped by the river. My mother was a good cook and decided we could have pigeon pie. She cut up the pigeons and cooked them slowly for a long time, but there were as tough as leather. Goodness knows how old they were – even our dog could not eat them.

My mother just sat and cried thinking about the good times we used to have before the war when the house was full of friends and relations all having a wonderful time. But later that day, my Dad, who was stationed in Knockholt in Kent, somehow managed to get home for a few hours, and we were all grateful to be together and alive.

STUFFED MUTTON

1 leg of mutton, or loin of mutton (half a leg does, but is more difficult to stuff).

Bone with a sharp carving knife, or get your butcher to do it. Spread the meat flat, stuff one end with your favourite savoury stuffing, the other end with sausage meat, the two meeting in the centre. Fold meat over, re-forming into shape, sew with sacking needle and stout thread, place sewn side down in baking dish, spread liberally with dripping. Surround meat with halved potatoes, peeled or in jackets. Put them in the baking dish after the meat is partially cooked as they take less time than your joint. Allow about 40–50 minutes.

Dorothy Adcock wrote: 'I remember mum arguing with the butcher because he said he could only let her have a duck, and she said there was no meat on it. One year we had to make do with liver and onions.' Others, like W.J. Wheatley, were luckier: 'We kept chickens and my grandfather had poultry long before the war, so every Christmas and other high days and holidays throughout the war we did all right, we also had our own eggs. To obtain chicken feed from the corn merchants we had to give up our egg rations. We also collected scraps from a local hotel.' At one Shaftesbury Society children's home, Etherington Hall, the matron wrote: 'At breakfast there were new-laid boiled eggs, for dinner there was chicken. Such are the advantages of keeping hens!'

Roy Proctor remembers: 'We kept chickens, so we had one of the old hens. My mother steamed it first, then roasted it.' The *Radio Times* advised its readers: 'About the Christmas dinner. If you have only an old boiling fowl available, stand it on a trivet in a saucepan one-third filled with water, and steam gently for about 2 hours, according to weight: then, when it has cooked a little, stuff it and roast rather quickly in the oven for 45 minutes to 1 hour, covering it first with as much fat as you can muster.'

The Times reported: 'If there were not so many turkeys as usual it was satisfactory to learn that roast turkey was on the Christmas Day menu in the decorated wards of the London hospitals. Some patients at University College Hospital actually had bananas, two bunches of which were left with the porter for them by an anonymous benefactor in Merchant Navy uniform. The bananas were wrapped in a copy of the *Miami Daily News* of 15 December.'

The Ministry of Food suggested various alternatives to a bird. One was a recipe for stuffed mutton, which the Ministry insisted was 'with apple or bread sauce . . . as delicious as any turkey!'

A lucky few were able to get the traditional goose. Mike Owen recalled: 'I was fortunate enough to have an uncle who kept geese, and every year at Christmas he would provide us with our Christmas dinner. As a young child the sight of this bird hanging on the cellar stairs (unplucked) was frightening. My father with a sack across his knee would pluck the goose, small feathers filling the air with every pluck!' And of course there was the black market. Margaret Peers remembers: 'At Christmas my mother would go to a shop in Breck Road, Everton, called Sturgen's, and she would wait 'til they closed, and you could get a goose for 12s 6d which was a lot of money in those days.' Most people were far more likely to dine on 'mock goose' that year.

Vera Sibley wrote: 'As we got near Christmas, things were hoarded like sugar and dried egg to make some sort of cake or pudding.'

MOCK GOOSE

1½lb potatoes
2 large cooking apples
4oz cheese
half teaspoon dried sage
Salt and pepper
three-quarters of a pint of vegetable stock
1 tablespoon flour

Slice potatoes thinly, slice apples, grate cheese. Grease fireproof dish, place in it a layer of potatoes, cover with apple and a little sage, season lightly and sprinkle with cheese. Repeat, leaving potatoes and cheese to cover. Pour in half a pint of stock, cook in a moderate oven for 45 mins. Blend flour and remaining stock, pour into dish and cook another 15 mins. Serve as a main dish with green vegetables.

MINISTRY OF FOOD 'CHRISTMAS FRUIT PIES'

This mixture is a good alternative to mincemeat.

Warm 1 teaspoonful marmalade (or jam, but this is not so spicy) in a small saucepan over tiny heat. Add ¼lb prunes (soaked for 24 hours, stoned and chopped) or other dried fruit, 1 tablespoonful sugar, 1 teacupful stale cake crumbs (or half cake, half breadcrumbs), ½ teaspoonful mixed spice. Stir together until crumbs are quite moist. Remove from heat, add 1 large chopped apple; also some chopped nuts if you have any. Make up into small pies or large open flans. The mixture keeps several days in a cool place.

Many pundits suggested carrot cake instead of Christmas cake, or a sponge cake made with no butter or margarine. Grace Newsom recalled: 'Cakes were made with liquid paraffin in place of fat, dried egg, and green twigs from the hedgerow in place of angelica, which we made sure were removed before the cake was cut!' Apparently the paraffin cake tasted all right, but often had unfortunate after-effects: 'for the next few hours you had to stay near a toilet'.

Christmas cakes would, of course, be covered in mock marzipan.

Even mock marzipan was not so easy to get. As Robina Hinton pointed out: 'Soya flour made good marzipan with a drop of almond essence – first find the essence!' Patricia McGuire remembers: 'We had cooking lessons at school and for Christmas made a dessert of junket, which was a sort of blancmange (if it set!). Mine never did, and by the time I arrived home I had lost most of it. We had also made mock marzipan holly leaves from some sort of semolina concoction and that was about all I

MOCK MARZIPAN

½lb haricot beans
4 tablespoons sugar
2 tablespoons ground rice
1 teaspoon almond essence
1 tablespoon margarine

Soak the beans for 24 hours, then cook until tender in fresh, unsalted water. Put them on a tin in a warm oven to get dry and floury. Rub them through a sieve. Beat the sugar into the bean puree, add the ground rice, warmed margarine and, finally, the flavouring. Beat until smooth. Any flavouring or colouring may be added.

arrived home with.' Dorothy Adcock vividly recalls 'rock-hard dried milk icing and soya marzipan on the cake'.

When jelly was unavailable, the Ministry advised housewives to mix gelatine with the sweetened juice from bottled or tinned fruit. Dorothy Adcock wrote: 'I remember tasteless jellies made with fruit squash and so solid it had to be chewed.'

MINISTRY OF FOOD 'EMERGENCY CREAM'

Bring ½ pint of water to blood heat, melt 1 tablespoonful unsalted margarine in it. Sprinkle 3 heaped tablespoonfuls house-hold milk powder into this, beat well, then whisk thoroughly. Add 1 teaspoonful sugar and 1 teaspoonful vanilla. Leave to get cold.

But even if the table was rather bare, you could still brighten up your home for the festivities. *Picture Post* reported: 'Even at this fourth wartime Christmas, you could still get a good glitter by buying here and there and pooling old stocks.' The *Radio Times* said: 'Christmas trees are scarce and very expensive, and imitation ones prohibitive in price, so a few carefully cherished flowers or small sprays of holly will, I expect, provide the Christmas

Even bottle stoppers were in short supply. The shortage of rubber meant few balloons among the decorations that year.

decorations in most homes.' Alternatively you could make your own tree. Grace Newman remembers collecting old, blown light-bulbs from friends and neighbours for several months before December. 'Then my sister and I painted them with some old silver paint. When that was dry we painted stars and so on, in black. Then we hung them from the tree using cotton. They made really good Christmas tree baubles.'

Stitchcraft magazine that December gave instructions for making both the tree and the decorations. The tree decorations included the angel on top, a 'motor wagon' made from a matchbox, a flower basket, drinking mugs, a yacht, a lamb, a horse and cart, and a lobster. The ensemble was finished off with 'daisy-chains': 'Cut any number of small flower shapes about the size of a shilling. Paint these in bright colours, then thread them alternately with either bugle beads or chopped hollow corn-stalks. If you have neither of these use coloured string and make a knot each side of the flower to keep it in place.'

The Ministry of Food also tried to be festive: 'A Christmassy sparkle is easy to [obtain using] sprigs of holly or evergreen for use on puddings. Dip your greenery in a strong solution of Epsom salts. When dry it will be beautifully frosted.' With paper shortages, decorations became makeshift. Some were as basic as twigs dipped in whitewash. People cut shapes from coloured paper and strung them on to cotton (tissue paper or sweet wrappers were favourite materials if you could get them). Other types of decoration were equally crude. In January the Ministry of Supply had prohibited the manufacture of many rubber goods, including children's balloons. They might be replaced with pieces of holly, shrubs or any available greenery, decorated with glass balls, pine cones, apples, and assorted homemade decorations. Still in determinedly festive mood the Ministry of Food announced, that although there were 'no gay bowls of fruit' to decorate the table, 'vegetables have such jolly colours. The cheerful glow of carrots, the rich crimson of beetroot, the emerald of parsley – it looks as delightful as it tastes.'

On 18 December the *Radio Times* advised 'Christmas this year must be a practical affair with only necessary and carefully chosen gifts for those

HOMEMADE CHRISTMAS TREE AND DECORATIONS

To make the tree:

Roll a tube of thick paper, any colour, like this (about 28in long by 2½in diameter, with about eight slits cut in from each end, about 2in long). The ends, snipped down for two inches, are bent outwards for the base and inwards for the tip later on. Glue firmly in position along the long edge and paint any bright colour. (This forms the trunk.)

Now make different-sized squares of paper, the largest fifteen inches square, and the smallest six inches square. Roll these into cone shapes, glue in position, and paint green. When dry, fix to trunk (with a few stitches at the top) with fine twine or linen thread. Use a sharp needle that will pass through the tube easily without bending it out of shape. Cover main trunk in this way, the small cones at the top and the large ones at the bottom, working up from the base. Paint a few white or silver spots here and there on the cones, or, if you have any silver frost, stick on some of that instead.

Finish off the top (of the trunk) by gluing together the slits at one end very firmly so that they form a point to be gathered together at the top by a big ribbon bow. This tip is also painted green or the shade of the main trunk.

Spread out the feet slits at right angles to trunk, and tack or glue firmly to a six-inch square of either thick cardboard or plywood. Over these feet paste other pieces of paper to strengthen, then paint thickly over this base, using several coats. (*Stitchcraft*)

closest to us, and whenever possible a communal Christmas dinner shared by branches of a family or friends.' Jones & Higgins of Peckham advertised that 'Father Christmas is here, but he is unable to bring the usual amount of large toys.' *Stitchcraft* magazine declared: 'There will be few toys in the shops this Christmas, but there is no reason why you should not have plenty on the family tree, provided you are ready to spend a little time and thought on making them'. Paul Fincham recalled: 'By Christmas 1942 new toys and games just never appeared. I had Meccano sets, a conjuring set, and a chemistry set, all of which were snapped up at once when I advertised them locally, as were jigsaws, even with a few pieces missing, and books (especially annuals) which looked distinctly second-hand!'

The same Ministry of Supply Order that had prohibited the manufacture of children's balloons also affected many other rubber goods, including various toys. It also licensed the manufacture of rubber footballs (and other 'ball bladders'), tennis and golf balls, etc., leading to further shortages of gifts available. Available presents for children

Aircraft kits, such as these by 'Truscale', could still be bought, and not only of British aircraft, there were our new US allies' planes and even *Luftwaffe* models.

included doll's bed sets, consisting of a blanket, sheet, pillow-case and art silk eiderdown (12in by 17in) at 10s 6d; dressed dolls 'with sleeping eyes' for 35s 6d, a 26in-long wooden railway engine at 12s 11d, Morse code tapper sets for 8s 6d, and metal paintboxes for 4s 6d.

Suggested gifts for adults included bath salts in a glass container for 7s 6d, coloured spills in a holder for 3s 3d, cork tablemat sets for 6s 11d, men's leather braces for 8s 3d (or in webbing for 6s 8d), men's leather slippers from 15s 11d to 19s 11d (plus four coupons), and ladies' velvet slippers, with soft leather soles and Cuban heels, for 8s 11d (three coupons). Coupons were a big problem. Even the classic present of a box of four handkerchiefs required one coupon, no matter if they were children's (embroidered in one corner) for 3s 9d, adults' white cotton, also embroidered, for 4s 7d, or lace-edged for 7s 5d. Men's all-wool ties at 2s 6d also required one coupon. Freeman Brothers of Crofton Park advertised 'many one-coupon presents in stock'. If coupons were not a problem, you could buy Dad a pair of Union flannel pyjamas in 'fancy blue, fawn and grey stripes for 24s 6d and 8 coupons'.

There were, of course, the usual instructions for homemade gifts, although these were becoming far more unusual, and also more inventive, as raw materials became ever scarcer. *Stitchcraft* carried the usual knitting patterns for babies' clothes, 'three-coloured gloves', cardigans, and even fair-isle slippers, plus 'a crocheted sailor cap', as well as instructions for a bag 'made from strips of ribbon'.

A whole range of goods now required precious clothing coupons.

You could still get expensive gifts, of course. One furrier (furs were not included in the rationing system and were therefore coupon free) was advertising mink wallaby and squirrel coney from 10 guineas, Mole Coney from 8 guineas and Beaver Coney from 7 guineas. More modestly there were silver foxes from 3 guineas, and foxes from £2.

Bouquets of flowers became rare as it had become illegal to send them by rail. Parcels could still be sent, but British Railways pleaded: 'Fewer

MATCH-HOLDER FOR CHILDREN TO MAKE

Materials: Odd pieces of old paper in strips, half-inch wide, and rather larger strips one-and-three-quarter inches wide. Six-and-a-half inches of emery or sandpaper, about one inch wide. Some glue and brightly coloured enamel paints. A fine steel knitting needle, or something similarly thin and strong.

To make: wrap narrow strips of paper round and round the tip of the knitting needle, gluing it each time you go round to keep it smooth and firm. When this circle is about one-and-a-half inches across, take the wide strips of paper and wind them round the first circle in the same way, but so that one end of this wider circle is hollow to make the stand. [In case you've lost the plot at this point, as I did when I first read the instructions, you first make a disc by winding the thin paper, then add the thicker paper, forming a sort of tube with a solid base.]

When this [outer] circle is about one-eighth of an inch wide, use small strips again and go on winding and gluing away to make the stand another quarter-of-an-inch bigger. [It has now become a sort of top hat shape, but open at the top.]

Rub the bottom of the stand until it is quite smooth, then paint the base in any bright colour you have. Next glue sandpaper round the wide part of the stand [to make a match-striker], and lastly, paint the top above the sandpaper and inside in another bright shade of enamel.

Many presents were now homemade, and not only the traditional jumper or socks, now you could make your own jewellery, as this item from *Needlewoman & Needlecraft* shows.

Christmas Parcels please! Christmas parcels must on no account hold up vital war traffic. Before deciding to send a parcel, ask yourself "Is it really necessary?" The railways must carry service personnel, weapons and munitions in every available coach, truck and wagon this Christmas.' Some of the best parcels came from abroad. Roy Proctor recalled: 'We got food parcels from Australia as my brother was in the forces out there. There was butter in tins, dried fruit, chocolate, and other things.'

Commercially produced cards could sometimes be obtained but many chose to make their own.

Those for friends or relatives serving overseas might have to be sent as early as August. Even those for inland delivery had to be posted early. The Post Office issued its normal appeal:

Post your Christmas letters and parcels early – earlier than you have ever done before. This Christmas the Post Office will have to face one of the hardest it has ever had. Still more of its skilled staff have left for service with the forces, and the reserves of labour, transport and accom-modation normally available have been depleted in the interests of the war effort.

To ensure delivery by Christmas Day all classes of correspondence should be posted a clear week before Christmas and postings must be completed, at the latest, by Saturday December 19th.

An alternative to sending cards was to telephone. In recent years Christmas calls have been cheap, or even free, but not in 1942. The GPO announced: 'The cheap evening rate for trunk calls will be suspended on Christmas Day, Boxing Day and the following Sunday. That is, full (day) rates will be in operation from 5am on December 25th until 7pm on December 28th. It is hoped that telephone traffic will be so reduced that the bulk of telephone staff can spend part of the Christmas week-end at home.'

That year the Shaftesbury Society entertained 15,000 needy guests for Christmas dinner. Parties were thrown by many other groups, too. The following report from the *Kentish Mercury* beautifully sums up so many of the Christmas parties given by the Civil Defence Services for local children:

Randall Place, Greenwich, Heavy Rescue Party entertained 130 children on Saturday [12 December]. The main event of the afternoon was a cine-matograph programme in the Williamson Memorial Hall (lent by Mr Brooke). After tea each child received a toy (made by the Heavy Rescue Service personnel) together with lollipops, apples and a new threepenny bit. Popular songs were played by Mr Newble on his accordion during tea.

Last year, thanks to the warning we issued about the shortage of books—and thanks to the heed that was paid to it — most of our customers were able without undue difficulty to make a satisfactory selection for their Christmas presents.

Finding gifts took time – this advertisement for WH Smith from 7 November urges its readers to start looking immediately.

The Times reported:

Christmas parties and entertainments, turkeys and toys, have been provided for British children on an almost lavish scale by American and Canadian and other troops. Most of the toys on the Christmas trees at the Canadian parties were made by the soldiers themselves in their spare time out of scrap wood and metal. Americans have forgone their own supplies of turkey to make them over to British children, besides subscribing generously for their entertainment.

Home Service programmes on Christmas Day included *Christmas Post 1942*, described as 'an outside broadcast featuring Wynford Vaughan Thomas and postman Grubb delivering letters in a London street'; *Music While You Work*, played by the band of the Manchester Regiment; *The Channel Islands*, a programme with music; and *Break for Music*, an ENSA concert for war workers. As always the Empire link-up programme was broadcast at 2 p.m.

Entitled *The Fourth Christmas*, it began in Britain with a Christmas party for Maltese children; then moved to a port in north-east England to meet Free French, Norwegian, Polish, Dutch, Belgian, Greek, Czech and 'Jugo-Slavian' troops stationed in Britain. The next section was from abroad, with messages from our allies in America, Russia and China, then from servicemen in Canada, Australia, New Zealand, India and South Africa, and a party for US troops in Britain. Finally it went to a thanksgiving service in Cairo Cathedral.

Reflecting the public mood, the King's Christmas speech emphasised confidence in the future:

With a shortage of suitable gifts a National Savings Certificate was not only patriotic, it was available!

This year it adds to our happiness that we are sharing it with so many of our comrades in arms from the United States of America. . . . The recent victories won by the United Nations enable me this Christmas to speak with firm confidence about the future. . . . Tremendous blows have been struck by the armies of the Soviet Union . . . The lessons learned during the forty tremendous months behind us have taught us how to work together for victory, and we must see to it that we keep together after the war to build a worthier future.

At 4.30 came *Children Calling Home*, which allowed British evacuee children to call home, and also enabled American and Canadian children to call their

WHEN THE LIGHTS GO ON AGAIN
(ALL OVER THE WORLD)
BY
EDDIE SEILER
SOL MARCUS
BENNIE BENJEMEN

IRWIN DASH MUSIC CO. LTD. · 17 BERNERS ST. LONDON W.I.

1/- NET.

The mood had changed, and so had the music. There was no question now that Britain and her Allies would win, it was just a question of when.

fathers serving with the US and Canadian forces in this country. In the evening there was a *Christmas Party at the Freedom Club*, which was 'the first Christmas Day party in this country' for men who had escaped from occupied Europe. At 8pm came the nation's favourite: Tommy Handley in ITMA, followed by *The Plot to Overthrow Christmas*, described as a 'seasonable extravaganza for broadcasting', and the evening finished with Henry Hall and his Orchestra.

Alternatives on the Forces programme included a Sunday service 'for isolated units', *Christmas Dinner on a Minesweeper*, the Canadian Army Christmas Concert, the Dance Orchestra of the Royal Air Force, and *Vera Lynn's Christmas Card*. Vera Lynn had one of the musical hits of the year, with 'Yours'. Other popular songs included 'When the lights go on again (All Over the World)', 'You're in my arms (and a million miles away)', and Disney's 'Little April Showers', but without doubt the biggest hit of the season was 'White Christmas' from the film *Holiday Inn*.

The newsreels showed the usual fare of the boys in the forces, this time in the Middle East, with footage of soldiers singing carols in the desert. W.J. Wheatley remembers: 'The song "White Christmas" was very popular at Christmas 1942. I went to the cinema with my father and the newsreel showed some of our victories in the Western Desert, columns of Axis prisoners and smiling British Tommies in the searing heat. The background music was "White Christmas". That for some

CHRISTMAS PRESENT TO THE FORCES

Our men at the front cannot relax this Christmas. Nor must you. There can be no truce, no armistice in the Battle for Fuel. Fuel savers have done well in the last few months. Any slackening off now in the saving of coal, coke, electricity, gas, paraffin – even for a couple of days – would lose much of the ground we have just gained. There's no need for a cold, cheerless Christmas. But there IS need to make sure that this Christmas will not lead to forgetfulness about fuel saving. The best Christmas present we can give our fighting forces is to keep on saving fuel so as to give them more weapons.

CHRISTMAS ACTION HINTS

1. Don't 'roar' your resources of coal away; and don't 'let yourself go' on gas and electric fires. Colder weather is coming.
2. Don't forget that water is precious – especially hot water. Don't wash up in 'dribs and drabs'. Collect a decent pile of crockery and make one job of it.
3. Above all, share your firesides. It's the get-together season and by getting together round one fire, two or three families can keep really warm and comfortable and still keep their fuel consumption low.
4. Send a card to the Public Relations Branch, Ministry of Fuel and Power, Dean Stanley Street, London S.W.1, for advice on how to lag your pipes and tanks.

FUEL SAVERS – FIGHT ON

The Ministry of Fuel and Power exhorted everyone to fight on in the battle to save fuel.

reason always stuck in my mind.' Government shorts included *Eat more Spuds* and *Keep an eye on your fuel and save, save, save. Fashion Hints*, featuring Anne Edwards, the fashion editor of *Woman* magazine, showed how to use scraps of material to make a patchwork waistcoat and coat, and how to turn one old hat into two new ones using some netting.

British films on release included Flanagan and Allen in *We'll Smile Again*, described as 'a film studio spy extravaganza'. Also on release was *Went the Day Well*, a classic propaganda piece showing a British village sturdily repulsing an attempted take-over by German commandos. For those who liked musicals, there was Arthur Askey in *King Arthur was a Gentleman*, with Ann Shelton. US productions included *The Magnificent Dope*, a comedy with Henry

Fonda, Lynn Bari, Don Ameche and Edward Everett Horton, and *The Road to Morocco* with the usual team of Bob Hope, Bing Crosby and Dorothy Lamour. Propaganda pieces included *All Through the Night*, starring Humphrey Bogart as a Damon Runyonesque gangster who takes on fifth-columnists led by Peter Lorre and Conrad Veidt, *Pied Piper* with Monty Wooley as a grumpy old man caught up in the German invasion of France, who collects about him refugee children including Roddy McDowall, and of course the classic *Mrs Miniver* with Greer Garson and Walter Pidgeon. Abbott and Costello starred in the comedy thriller *Who Done It?*, while in a musical vein Ann Sothern and Red Skeltern starred in another of the Maisie series, *Maisie Gets Her Man*. For the children there was *Bambi*, described as 'a great love story as only Disney can tell it'.

A wide range of pantomimes was on offer that year. *Dick Whittington* was being performed in Norwich, Glasgow and Worcester, among other places, while *Cinderella* could be seen at the Stoll, with Fay Compton in the title role and Ted Ray as Buttons, along with Nervo and Knox, and Naughton and Gold. It was also being performed in Ipswich, Bristol, Bradford, Preston and Edinburgh. *Babes in the Wood* was on at the Darlington, while *Aladdin* appeared at Sheffield and Cardiff. *Red Riding Hood* was on in Manchester and *Bo-Peep* at Salford. *Sleeping Beauty* reposed at the Blackpool Old Hall, while *Mother Goose* could be seen at the Swansea Empire and also at the London Coliseum, where Patricia Burke starred, along with 'Kirby's flying ballet [who] grace the scenes of fairyland'. *Robinson Crusoe* was on in Burnley and Glasgow, *Puss in Boots* was at the Newcastle Palace Theatre, and Arthur Askey, Florence Desmond and Eddie Gray were in *Jack and Jill* at His Majesty's Theatre. The latter had a good write-up: 'The dancing is well disciplined and the "50 beautiful girls" live tolerably well up to their labels.' *Peter Pan* was at the Winter Garden Theatre, with Ann Todd in the leading role and Alastair Sim as Captain Hook.

There were, of course, other shows. At the Tower Ballroom, Blackpool, for example, there was a children's ballet entitled *Santa Claus Comes to*

Town, while at the Scala you could see the Sanger Brothers' Circus, but minus their lions and tigers – apparently the authorities had decided that they would constitute 'an air-raid risk'!

On Christmas Day a crowd of 14,621 watched Tottenham Hotspur draw 1–1 with Brentford, that season's winner of the London War Cup. As so many top-class players were serving in the forces, much of the play was less skilful, but more goals were scored. That Christmas the Football League North champions Blackpool beat Blackburn 7–2, Everton beat Manchester City 6–3, Lincoln beat Notts County 8–1, Bury beat Rochdale 7–3, and Crewe beat Wrexham 8–2, but the biggest goal tally of all came in the Newcastle v. Gateshead game, which ended 6–6. These teams are all still represented in today's fixture lists but there were others which no longer survive. In the League West, for example, Lovell's Athletic beat Aberaman 5–0. The team from a Welsh toffee factory, Lovell's went on to be the League West champions for the following two seasons.

On Boxing Day 323,000 people watched the opening Football War Cup qualifying matches, paying an average of 1*s* 3*d* to get in. Some 12,500 watched Brentford beat Tottenham Hotspur 2–1, while in the North Eastern League Cup Final Aberdeen beat Dunfermline Athletic 6–1.

There was no horse-racing in England that Christmas, punters being forced to look to Leopardstown and Limerick for their entertainment. Alternatively, there was greyhound racing at many tracks in London; on Boxing Day there was a plethora of meetings, at Catford, Harringay, Stamford Bridge, West Ham, Charlton, Hendon, Walthamstow, White City, Clapton, New Cross, Wandsworth, Hackney Wick and Wembley, to name but a few.

CHRISTMAS WEDDINGS

Christmas leave sometimes meant Christmas weddings, as long-separated couples used their short time together to tie the knot. These were often short-notice affairs.

ARMY PHRASES

"Present Arms!"

Those service personnel who could be spared would be given Christmas leave, as shown in this cartoon from *Motor Cycling* magazine. It often became a time not only of celebration, but also of hastily improvised weddings.

By Christmas 1943 Betti Thomson had been engaged for nearly four years and had been apart from her fiancé for most of that time. She recalled: 'My parents and I were preparing for bed when the doorbell rang – who would be calling at this time of night? – was our blackout in order? My father went to the door. I heard exclamations of surprise, a voice I hadn't heard for so many years. It couldn't be – but it was! Frank was home again. He had a month's leave prior to joining his unit in East Anglia. His section of the Eighth Army had been brought back from the Middle East to prepare for the Second Front.'

Mrs Thomson went on to describe the preparations for the wedding. Her story gives a wonderful insight into the problems faced by couples getting married during the war:

What a lot of preparations had to be made. I managed to get time off from the Local Government Office in Bebington where I worked. Christmas was too near to be married before the 25th – we decided on the 29th after consultation with the minister of the church where we had met. With no petrol for private cars, we had to use buses and cars to commute between Frank's home in Prenton and ours in Bromborough and for visits to Liverpool where we managed to find a wedding ring. The licence was purchased.

The whole family went into action. First of all, what to wear? Frank's corporal's uniform was too disreputable to consider, although the buttons shone. Everyone pooled their clothing coupons and a suit was found. (He had broadened out so much that none of his civvy clothes fitted him.) How helpful the assistants were. A pale blue crêpe dress was found for me – I still have the buttons which are gold with a lion's head on them. The assistant kicked off her own high-heeled shoes so that I could wear them to get the effect of the dress and the hat she had produced from the millinery department. It was dark brown to match the shoes I already had. My bridesmaids were to be my younger sister and my future sister-in-law. My sister was a typical land girl, sturdy and a complete contrast in build to Frank's sister. Eventually identical burgundy dresses in different sizes were discovered – we breathed a sigh of relief. Flowers had to be chrysanths – there wasn't much choice.

With the Christmas cards went notes inviting guests to the wedding – lists were made and many phone calls. With the essentials catered for we could enjoy the festive season but I must admit it was a relief to have the shops open again and the bus services back to normal.

The wedding cake hadn't been forgotten. My future mother-in-law had saved the ingredients over the year and she had baked the cake before Christmas. She had saved some icing sugar too, but this had become so hard and lumpy that it needed careful sieving. I have a feeling soya flour was used in almond paste. It was iced by a friend who worked in a bakery and one evening Frank and I set out to collect it from her home. The bus was full up downstairs so we negotiated the steep stairs up to the top deck only to find that was full too. Crouching down at the back, partly sitting on one of the seats, we hoped we wouldn't be discovered and all was well.

If anyone deserved a medal it was my mother. After all the cooking she had done for Christmas now she embarked on a marathon task. How good people were. Little gifts of a packet of tea, some sugar, a tin of fruit, a slab of margarine, etc., kept arriving. Eventually an almost pre-war spread was achieved.

Betti Thomson and her husband Frank at their wedding, Christmas 1943.

On the morning of the 29th all was ready. I remember the quietness of the sunny, frosty morning as I waited with my father for the hired car to arrive. All went well, especially the reception at home. How people enjoyed a celebration and exciting eats in those days. We tried to talk to everyone and to thank them for the presents they had found for us at such short notice. When it was time for us to leave for our train they were so engrossed that we slipped out almost unnoticed.

We had decided on London for our honeymoon. There had been no air-raids for some time and in wintertime it seemed a good choice. The hotel was all we could have wished for and although museums and other places of interest were closed the shops had more variety than at home and we had meals out and went to the theatre. What marvellous shows we saw – I still have the programmes which include Ivor Novello in *The Dancing Years* and Fay Compton in *No Medals*.

Incidentally the bill for seven nights at the hotel was £12 5s and this included at least one evening meal as well as bed and breakfast.

Patricia McGuire also recalled a Christmas-time wedding:

The thing I remember most was a Boxing Day wedding in about 1942. The bride had a white dress more grey-looking than white as it had been used so many times before, nevertheless she looked lovely. The groom had his Royal Navy uniform on. The bridesmaids were all dressed in red crêpe paper, but they also looked very pretty. The thing that sticks in my mind the most was the reception. We didn't know what was in the sandwiches, mostly vegetables and a sort of concoction made with dried egg. Best of all was the wedding cake. It looked superb and we were all eager to sample it. When the time came to cut the lovely three-tier cake everybody crowded round; what a disappointment – the outer layer lifted off to reveal the tiniest cake possible. I think we got a mouthful each.

Margaret Cushion's sister was married on Boxing Day 1941:

In 1941 I was seventeen and my sister Elizabeth was twenty. We lived in Liverpool by the docks, not far from Scotland Road. Her fiancé Henry was in the Navy. They decided to get married on Boxing Day, and he got a few days' leave. The wedding was all set for 3 o'clock in St Alban's Church, which was just around the corner. We had to get everything prepared on Christmas Day. We had to make sandwiches, bake scones and apple pie, and make a trifle. Although we were on rations, all the neighbours chipped in because it was a small, close-knit community.

When everything was ready, it had to be taken over to the air-raid shelter, which was in one of the arches under the railway. Our nights were spent in the shelters until it was light – it was our nightly routine. Of course, it was very poorly lit, we had no gas or 'lecky' [electricity] at the time so we had to borrow as many paraffin oil lamps as we could to light it.

The wedding went very well. Once the ceremony was over, it was straight to the shelter for the eats and beer, which was in quart bottles in those days.

Christmas 1943

•

Many of our friends Overseas can have no Christmas gifts this year.

Yet we shall remember them.

Can we make a better gift than prayer for absent ones?

Can we remember them more appropriately than by supporting the work that is costing them so much?

SEND US SOME OF YOUR CHRISTMAS GIFTS.

Methodist Missionary Society   25, Marylebone Road, London, N.W.1.

FIVE

—— 1943 ——

The Fifth Christmas

By now some people were finding Christmas a painful reminder that the war had dragged on for another year. In spite of this, many people felt that this just might be the last wartime Christmas. The editorial of that year's *Motor Cycling* magazine pointed out:

'A Merry Christmas and a Happy New Year', expressed in December 1939, suggested a form of wishful thinking only exceeded in its irony by the same greeting in December 1940, when the outlook was black in the extreme. Now, however, in this, the fifth, Christmas period of the war, it is possible to give the fine old traditional greeting to our readers at home and overseas in the sincere belief that the wishes may come true. While it would be presumptuous to suggest that this may be the last wartime Christmas, there is at least reasonable cause to hope that in twelve months' time peace on earth may have become a reality.

Home Chat magazine commented: 'Santa Claus – that incurable old optimist – is filling up his sack again and combing out his white beard, and putting on his very best festive smile, because I believe he knows that we shan't have to wait so very long now for that Christmas when we shall all be together again with the person or persons who matter most in our separate little world.'

This confidence in our eventual victory was clearly displayed in January 1943, when the Allies had agreed that they would accept nothing less than the total unconditional surrender of the Axis countries. In May German resistance in North Africa came to an end and that same month

TRIUMPH

Sends Greetings

TO ALL
MOTOR-
CYCLISTS
IN THE ARMED
FORCES AND THOSE
ENGAGED ON THE
HOME FRONT

May the coming
year see a
successful
ending to your
War Efforts and
bring with it a return
to the freedom of the road,
which you enjoyed in the happier days of peace.

TRIUMPH ENGINEERING COMPANY LIMITED COVENTRY

Triumph motor cycle Christmas greeting from *Motor Cycling* magazine, December 1943.

Mussolini resigned. In July Allied forces had landed in Sicily, which fell in just thirty-eight days, and from there an invasion of mainland Italy was launched on 3 September. On the same day the Italian government surrendered unconditionally, although German forces in the country continued to put up heavy resistance. Yet one of our enemies was now defeated.

By December Allied forces were advancing up the mainland of Italy, finally capturing the mountain stronghold of Monte Cassino on the 7th, but they were becoming bogged down in the winter mud. Russian forces also continued their remorseless advance, while on Boxing Day news was received that the German battleship *Scharnhorst* had been sunk by the Royal Navy off the coast of Finland.

The Allied air assault was growing steadily stronger. During December RAF and USAAF aircraft dropped over 4,000 tons of bombs on Berlin alone, while on the 20th the RAF dropped 2,000 tons of bombs on Frankfurt, and on Christmas Eve some 2,000 aircraft attacked the coastal areas of northern France. In contrast, the easing-off of raids by the *Luftwaffe* on Britain had continued; 2,200 tons of bombs were dropped on Britain over the course of the year (just over 10 per cent of the 1941 figure), and nearly 2,400 civilians had been killed. *The Times* wrote: 'For the home-based population it was one of the most peaceful of wartime Christmases. Reassuringly, at twelve-hour intervals came bulletins such as

"During the hours of daylight there has been nothing to report" or "Up to 7 o'clock this morning there has been no enemy air activity".'

Some 4¼ million men and 450,000 women were now serving in the forces, while over the course of the year more than 25,000 British servicemen had fallen into enemy hands.

That year the bells again summoned the people to church. *Picture Post* described St Paul's Cathedral on Christmas Eve: 'Many of the Londoners who sit in this congregation have come from the suburbs year after year to attend this annual celebration. In war time, despite the blackout and difficulties of travel, they still come from Tottenham and Clapham.' *The Times* reported that 'Christmas Day congregations in the churches were often large, sometimes even crowded. Mingled among the civilians were many uniformed men and women of the British Dominion, and allied services. Most numerous among those last were Americans.'

The RAF weather summary for Britain on Christmas Day read: 'South-westerly winds, light at first becoming moderate later. Much cloud with considerable fog in early morning.'

The war against the U-boats was at last being won. In the previous twelve months shipping losses had fallen to 3.1 million tons and by now levels of rationing were pretty well set. The only differences from the previous December were that the sugar and preserves rations were combined and could be taken as any combination of either, and cheese was down to 3oz (12oz special). Powdered eggs had been restricted to one packet per month after July, but in December 'Food Facts' pronounced: 'Now, as a special treat, we're to have a double ration of eggs – dried eggs – for the next four weeks! Make the very most of this bountiful supply and give your family delicious Christmas fare that smacks of pre-war days!' One other restriction lifted that Christmas was that 'wrinkled peas, whether or not steeped or soaked in water, will be sold free from points from December 12'. Another change was that furniture had begun to be rationed.

Transport was even more restricted than ever. London Transport announced that on Christmas Day the underground system would run

"*I just haven't got the Transport*"

Battles do not stop for Christmas. In this fifth winter of the War it is more than ever necessary that there should be no delay in the transport of war equipment for the services.

SEND FEWER PARCELS THIS CHRISTMAS

and make no unnecessary journeys

RAILWAY   EXECUTIVE   COMMITTEE

Donner and Blitzen, or perhaps Dasher and Dancer, are pulling the field gun in the background, so Father Christmas cannot move his sleigh – a joint plea to send fewer parcels and make no unnecessary journeys from the Railway Executive Committee.

a Sunday service until 4 p.m. and then trains would run at 'widened intervals'. There would be no buses, trams or trolley-buses at all after 4 p.m. and no country service buses all day.

The *Radio Times* on 17 December begged 'a word in time about your Christmas salvage. There is bound to be rather more of it than usual, however austere your festivities may be. String and paper from parcels, packing of all sorts, the bones from the turkey, the metal tops of bottles, those extra periodicals you buy for holiday reading, all the litter left about the room after the party – they are all wanted again, urgently. Sort them out carefully and put them in the proper receptacles as a Boxing-Day gift to the salvage campaign.'

On the 22nd the government announced that only one family in ten would get turkey or goose that Christmas. Vere Hodgson noted: 'We are pretty well on our beam ends as far as Christmas fare is concerned. No chance of turkey, chicken or goose – not even the

'Go easy with the soda', advert for Sparklets soda siphons – not an encouragement to drink more spirits – chance would be a fine thing! – but to consume less generally.

despised rabbit. If we can get a little mutton that is the best we can hope for. A few Christmas puddings are about. There are shops with three puddings and 800 registered customers.' The *News Chronicle* reported 'large and small traders in London and the suburbs were busy yesterday devising schemes for a fair distribution of turkeys'. One large store had devised its own complicated points system: each member of a family registered with the store for all rationed commodities would receive fourteen points if they were registered for bacon, and eight points if they were registered for butter and preserves only. Totals for each family would be worked out, and those with the highest totals would get what turkeys were available. Other smaller shops used less complicated methods, and many simply supplied their oldest customers first.

Patricia McGuire remembers: 'If you could get hold of a rabbit for a meal it was very special. I had an uncle who reared tame rabbits which were even tastier than the wild ones and my mother being an excellent cook used to do all sorts with them. I didn't know what I was eating, but enjoyed it. One particular Christmas I saw him bring the rabbit for our Christmas dinner which my mother would stuff and roast and I was horrified. Needless to say I was vegetarian that Christmas.' Joan Letts wrote: 'I remember Christmas 1943, which was a sombre occasion for our family. We went to Grandma's for lunch in the lounge with our parents, and had casseroled rabbit, while Great-Grandma, aged 92, was laid out in her coffin on the Morrison table shelter in the dining room. I was worried that we might have an air-raid and have to get under the table with the coffin on top.'

Home Chat magazine gave recipes for Christmas puddings: 'Though not up to the traditional standard of richness, Gladys Owen's puddings for the festive meal make the most of the good things available.'

Patricia McGuire still remembers 'so well the Christmas pudding my mother used to make which mostly consisted of carrots and apples and was very acceptable'.

It may surprise some people to find that the second of Gladys Owen's Christmas pudding recipes was a 'fruitarian' one, but

A WARTIME CHRISTMAS PUDDING

½lb each of flour, breadcrumbs, suet, carrots, potatoes, apples and dried fruits
two prepared dried eggs
two teaspoonfuls of pudding spice
one teaspoonful of bicarbonate of soda
half a pint of treacle or syrup
lemon flavouring or lime juice
a little milk or homemade wine

Mix together the flour, crumbs, chopped suet, spice and soda. Peel and chop the apples, and grate the carrots. Add them with the mashed potato, chopped fruit, and lemon flavouring to the other ingredients. Beat up the eggs, add the warmed syrup, then beat these well into the mixture. It should be just heavy enough to drop heavily from a spoon, so if too stiff add a little milk, or homemade wine. Put the mixture into one or two greased basins. Twist a piece of greased paper over the top and steam for about ten hours – five hours when they are made and five before serving them; or cover them with pudding cloths and boil for six to eight hours, merely heating them through before serving.

it must be remembered that vegetarianism had been popular in the 1930s.

It was still possible to decorate the Christmas cake. The confectionery department of Marshall & Snellgrove's in Oxford Street advertised various figures, including Father Christmas (in two sizes), polar bears, snowmen and a robin on a log, all for 1*s* to 1*s* 3*d* each. They also supplied artificial sprigs of mistletoe and holly at 1*s* and 6*d* respectively, and small coloured candles (9*d* a dozen) with floral

WARTIME MINCEMEAT

1½lb of chopped apples
4oz chopped suet
3oz chopped nuts
3oz dried fruit (any kind)
4oz golden syrup
one level teaspoonful each of ground ginger and pudding spice
lemon flavouring

Peel, core and chop the apples finely. Prepare the fruit, mincing it finely. Put the dry ingredients in a basin, add the lemon flavouring and syrup. Mix all well together and it is ready for use.

A FRUITARIAN CHRISTMAS PUDDING

½lb each of breadcrumbs and flour
1lb of dried fruits
¼lb each of sugar, pine kernels, and shelled nuts and almonds
2oz margarine
three dried eggs
two or more tablespoonfuls of lime juice cordial
4oz candied peel (if obtainable)

Pass the almonds and nuts through a mincing machine and chop the pine kernels coarsely. Prepare and chop the fruit. Put in a basin with the nuts, sugar, breadcrumbs and flour. Chop the peel coarsely and add it. Stir these well together, then add the melted margarine and lime juice cordial, and, lastly, the prepared and beaten eggs. Put the mixture in greased basins and cover with pudding cloths, put in a pan of boiling water and boil for six hours.

Soya flour can be added to the puddings in the proportion of one ounce to half a pound of flour.

holders in pink and white (4*s* a dozen). They also offered a sort of cardboard box decorated with plaster to look like an iced Christmas cake: 'these clever hoods, when placed over your fruit cakes, make them look for all the world like the iced cakes which appeared on our tables at Christmas-

Christmas returns again –

AND SOON, WE HOPE, WILL

IDRIS

QUALITY SOFT DRINKS

IDRIS LIMITED, LONDON, MAKERS OF QUALITY
BY APPOINTMENT TABLE WATERS THROUGH FIVE SUCCESSIVE REIGNS

time before the war. Sizes 7 inches in diameter and 3 inches deep, 4s 6d; 9 inches in diameter and 3 inches deep, 5s 6d; 10 inches in diameter and 4 inches deep, 7s 6d.' These could some-times cause disappoint-ment. Vera Sibley recalled: 'My father came home one day all triumphant with a chocolate cake, all decorated. When he undid it, it was cardboard, and under-neath was an eggless, fatless sponge – what a let-down!'

The Ministry of Food's 'Food Facts' offered assorted Christmas Recipes: 'Although they're strictly practical, they've all got that touch of glamour that must be there – or it isn't Christmas! You'll notice they're all made with eggs; and that's the reason they taste so good!' There followed recipes for a Christmas cake, almond biscuits, rainbow castles, carnival trifle, and tipsy sauce.

By Christmas 1943 many unavailable items were advertised, as looking forward to the day they would reappear, like this advert for Idris drinks.

A Touch of Christmas

THESE charming little decorations, which will help to cover up deficiencies in icing, all come from the Confectionery Dept., Marshall and Snelgrove, Oxford Street, London, W.1. Orders must not be less than one dozen assorted decorations, 1s. extra should be allowed on twelve decorations to cover postage, unless otherwise stated.

HERE'S Santa, himself, ready to do his share in making our war-time efforts look as festive as possible. He comes in two sizes. 1s. 3d. and 1s. respectively.

REMEMBER the snowman on the cake at Christmas when you were young? Of course you do, and the youngsters, to-day, will be just as thrilled as you were. The little fellow pictured here costs 1s. Polar Bears are just as popular, too. This one costs 1s.

ANOTHER memory from the past . . . the robin on the log. He is such a cheerful little bird, as bright and gay as ever, costing 12s. a dozen. Or if, in spite of all your efforts, your small son's incorrigibly war-minded, he'll adore the jolly battleship, 4½ inches long, price 1s. 3d.

THESE clever hoods, when placed over your fruit cakes, make them look for all the world like the iced cakes that appeared on our tables at Christmas-time before the War. Sizes 7 inches in diameter and 3 inches deep, 4s. 6d.; 9 inches in diameter, and 3 inches deep, 5s. 6d.; 10 inches in diameter and 4 inches deep, 7s. 6d. Post and packing 1s. 6d. extra. This can be bought separately.

SPRIGS of mistletoe with which to decorate the cake or a tiny Christmas tree. Price 12s. per dozen, post and packing. 9d.

THE matter of cakes and candles is a most important one. war-time or no. So this little box of coloured candles and the floral holders will be welcomed by many mothers of small children. The candles cost 9d. for a box of a dozen and the holders, in pink and white, 4s. a dozen. Candles and holders cannot be bought separately. The smallest order taken is for a dozen of each.

AND just because Christmas isn't Christmas without some holly about, here are some pretty little sprigs for the cake, 6s. a dozen. post 9d.

FOR where to buy see facing page. Remember that not less than one dozen decorations can be ordered, choosing your own assortment.

HOME CHAT

December 11th, 1943

Cake and other decorations from Marshall and Snelgrove in *Home Chat*. Especially interesting is the fake iced Christmas cake cover, which would go over a plain cake or sponge.

A few lucky individuals had special treats that year. *The Times* reported: 'Carrying gifts of oranges, lemons, grapes and bananas two hundred civilian workers from Gibraltar arrived in London on Christmas Eve to spend Christmas with their evacuated families.' (Some 12,000 evacuees from the island had come to Britain earlier in the war, when the island had seemed in danger of falling to the enemy.)

TIPSY SAUCE

Two dried eggs (dry); two level tablespoons flour; one level tablespoon sugar; five level tablespoons household milk (dry); one pint water; few drops of rum flavouring; ground nutmeg.

Method. Mix together dried eggs, flour, sugar and milk; blend with a little cold water to form a thin cream. Boil the rest of the water and, when boiling, pour slowly on egg mixture, stirring well all the time. Return to the pan; bring to the boil, and boil for 1–2 minutes. Add flavouring and grated nutmeg.

CARNIVAL TRIFLE

Make your trifle in the usual way, using little jam sandwiches if you haven't cake. Moisten with sweetened liquid from a bottle of fruit, or jam thinned with hot water. Use the Tipsy sauce recipe for your custard – this 'makes' the trifle. Decorate with grated chocolate, or crushed bottled sweets.

In an article entitled 'Christmas Comes Again', *Home Chat* magazine tried to encourage its readers:

Let us make the most of the Christmas that is almost upon us. Let us celebrate it by spreading as much happiness as we possibly can, and I do hope you haven't been prevented from making your yearly gifts to friends because of coupons and inflated prices.

My presents are ready . . . just odds and ends contrived from scraps of wool, such as egg-cosies, gloves, ration-card cases, to say nothing of string shopping bags.

That's one good thing the war has done, you know; it's made us quite thrilled to receive the humblest of gifts, and we really do value things because of the thought behind them and the effort they entailed, rather than for their splendour!

Last year I went into ecstasies of delight because some clever friend sent me a large packet of steel wool for cleaning my saucepans, while another kind soul sent me a tablet of bath soap (such self-denial!), and yet another a tin of custard powder, and it is these homely things, sent with our very best wishes, that are most appreciated these days.

Robina Hinton remembers the shortages: 'You had to make sure the Christmas shopping was done well before the season really started. The way things were, if you had money you spent it – you might be dead soon. So if you could get them you would spend your money on presents. Anything you could get – a bit of jewellery if you could, and stuff you get under the counter, you would hold on to for Christmas presents.'

Home Chat magazine made suggestions for suitable gifts:

Nowadays, the beauty gift is most elusive of all – and infinitely desirable. And still I'm making 'beauty' my present to many women friends this year – giving, instead of those luxury preparations, the more mundane toilet preparations which, because of their scarcity – their higher price – are precious now.

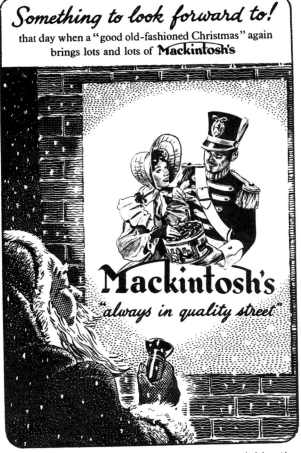

Something to look forward to!
that day when a "good old-fashioned Christmas" again brings lots and lots of **Mackintosh's**

Mackintosh's
"always in quality street"

Something else which was no longer available, the traditional Christmas gift of chocolates had disappeared with the introduction of sweet rationing.

Bath salts there are still – a real luxury now, for the small bottle costs twice or three times its pre-war price. Here I've found it more economical to buy one really big bottle, and this I'm dividing up, packing it into small jars the tops of which I've enamelled myself in gay colours. Some I've popped into dainty little bags I cut from scraps of organdie, or tied up in squares of Christmas paper saved from Christmases gone by.

Boxes of powder these days are a very 'safe' gift, for no longer are women ultra-particular that their powder has a particular perfume. . . . The box will come in its wartime wrapping, and here's where you can do wonders to make it gay and seasonable – wrapping it in a wee square of gay paper, or teaming it up with a chiffon or lace 'hankie' puff. They cost coupons to buy, so make the hankie from those scraps left from a dance frock, 'rolling' the edges finely and stitching a little wool puff in the centre.

Cold cream – hand cream – both will be welcome gifts – doubly welcome to the girl whose wartime job is taking a toll of her hands. And that reminds me, tuck in with the cream a pair of sleeping mitts – made from an odd scrap of soft silk.

The Service girl will be thrilled with a 'luxury' tablet of soap – if you've got a couple of soap-coupons to spare – to take her mind back to those leisurely baths of her civilian days. Team it with a face flannel – cut from the best part of an old towel, and blanket stitched in a dainty colour.

Advertised gifts included 'a pipe rack to hold four pipes in light oak for 9s 6d, a wicker and cane shopping basket decorated with raffia flowers for 9s 9d, or a bowl of artificial flowers for 21s. This advert from Chiesman's of Lewisham perfectly sums up the shortage of consumer goods: 'Special Offer – black grain football boots with studs, in sizes 6 to 10 only – a limited quantity only – unrepeatable offer – 24s 6d a pair.'

Women's magazines contained many examples of do-it-yourself presents: 'There's an unused cretonne curtain lying by. Then here's the gift for that housewife friend . . . a gay apron, its edges bound with matching bias', or 'Young sister, longing for new accessories for her winter coat, will thrill to a set of matching gloves and handbag. These you can stitch from an unrationed suede skin – or wash leather if you prefer it', or 'Bedroom slippers from gay felt, a wee ribbon bow for her frock centred with an old paste buckle, stream-lined cami-knicks cut from an old nightie, or a book jacket of strips of brilliant webbing.' And, of course, there were dolls, their faces, legs and arms made of old stockings and their bodies made of scrap material, or cuddly animals made of old velvet or odd bits of jersey.

Yvonne Pole remembers how homemade decorations could create a magical scene:

I lived with my mum and brother (Dad was killed at Singapore). Christmas morning we came down, the room was glowing with a lovely fire, and there was a small tree in the corner of the room. It had small cellophane bunches hanging from the branches. Inside were dolly mixtures, just a few, but effective; a few small candles in holders made the cellophane glisten and sparkle – it certainly was a magic room – we stood in amazement. There were also two socks, with an apple, a tangerine and a tin whistle – pure luxury. We were speechless!

Nita Luce remembers how one decoration almost led to disaster: 'I was born at the beginning of the war. We must have had Christmas trees as I spoilt Christmas 1943 for our family by eating a glass bauble off a tree – perhaps I thought it was a sweet.'

Christmas Day Home Service programmes included *Christmas Bells* from around Britain. The church bells rang again that Christmas, the general embargo on bell-ringing having been lifted in May, and of course the BBC was there to broadcast them. There was *Works Wonders*, in which munitions workers at a factory in Scotland entertained their colleagues with a concert, a *Christmas message* from the Archbishop of Canterbury, and at 2 p.m. *We Are Advancing*, described as 'this year's reunion programme'. This featured a soldier, a former prisoner of war, who was spending his first Christmas at home for five years; a US airbase where the airmen were entertaining their British counterparts; and messages from troops serving on the Alaska Highway and in South Africa, Brazil and New Guinea and its 'bitter jungle. A heartfelt greeting to the fighting men advancing there, slowly, painfully, but still advancing.' Then the programme moved on to Chungking, India, Bethlehem, Russia and, last of all, London.

As always these greetings were followed by the King's speech, in which he talked about absent loved ones:

> I hope that my words, spoken to them and to you, may be the bond that joins us all in company for a few moments on this Christmas Day. Since I last spoke to you many things have changed. But the spirit of our people has not changed. As we were not downcast by defeat, we are not unduly exalted by victory. . . . We know that much hard working and hard fighting, and perhaps harder working and harder fighting than ever before, are necessary for victory. We shall not rest from our task until it is nobly ended.

This was followed by *National Anthems of the Allies*. Later there was the brilliantly titled *Is your Genie really necessary?*, a satirical pantomime. For Children's Hour, it was that man again, Tommy Handley, in *Well, for Santa Claus*, followed by *A Christmas Day Unfairy Story*, with Dorothy Summers, Fred Yule, Sydney Keith, Bryan Herbert, Ronald, Chesney and Barrett, and Max Field.

In the evening came *Vaudeville of 1943* starring Randolph Sutton, Mr Murgatroyd and Mr Winterbottom, Robert Donat, Anne Ziegler and Webster Boothe, and Elsie and Doris Waters, followed by *Alice's Adventures in Wonderland* and a *Christmas Cabaret*, in which 'Carroll Gibbons, at the piano, invites you to join the party at the Merchant Navy Club'.

The Forces Programme, in addition to such old favourites as Sandy MacPherson and the Central Band of the Royal Air Force, included *ENSA Pulls the Crackers*, with Anna Neagle, Tessie O'Shea, Nancy Evans, James Woodburn and Sandy Powell, and *Rhythm of the Forces*, which consisted of music played by four Forces favourites. These favourites were Chuck Bills and his Armoured Force, The Blue Mariners Dance Band, The Dance Orchestra of the King's Royal Rifle Corps and The Dance Orchestra of No. 1 Balloon Centre. At 9.30 came *Command Performance*, a Christmas edition of the weekly programme by the 'Special Service Division of the

War Department of the United States of America'. The Master of Ceremonies was Bob Hope, and the programme included turns by Jack Benny, Fred Allen, Jimmy Durante, Nelson Eddy, Dinah Shore, Ginny Sims, Kay Kyser and his Orchestra, and Spike Jones and his City Slickers.

The *Columbia and Parlophone Record Guide* for December asked 'What can you buy these days that doesn't require coupons or points? Books, records . . . well, there isn't much else. Records give pleasure; there's no denying that the public during the war has realised the inestimable value and consolation of music and entertainment in recorded form.' There was one drawback, however. By now the purchase tax on records was over 60 per cent! Nevertheless there were plenty of new records released that Christmas. Columbia and Parlophone offered gift suggestions, starting with Malcolm Sargent conducting the Halle Orchestra playing *Fingall's Cave* on two 12-inch discs, or Muir Mathieson conducting the London Symphony Orchestra playing the *Warsaw Concerto* (each priced at 4*s*, plus 2*s* 7½*d* tax). On a lighter note they suggested humorous recordings such as Robb Wilton's 'The Munitions Worker' and 'The Home Guard', and Lucan and McShane in 'Old Mother Riley in the Police Force' (each priced at 4*s* 2*d* including tax).

For Christmas they recommended the BBC Chorus singing carols, and a compilation of Flanagan and Allen hits entitled 'Flanagan and Allen Successes'. Other popular records included the Band of His Majesty's Lifeguards playing 'Tommies' Tunes', and the Victor Silvester Jive Band's 'Stomping at the Savoy'. The children were not forgotten: 'Children love games, and in this respect the Parlophone set of "Singing Games for Children" are specially planned to enable kiddies of all ages to participate in the fun. The six records contain musically illustrated games which give children plenty of scope for acting a dozen different simple "charades".' The set, made by Chalmers Wood's Orchestra, cost a whacking 25*s*, including tax, but many parents probably thought that it was worth it for the chance of a little peace over the holiday. Meanwhile, HMV was advertising 'Nursery Rhymes and Carols' arranged by Uncle Mac, and recordings of music from various Walt Disney films.

Gift ideas from His Master's Voice included humorous recordings by Abbott and Costello, Arthur Askey, and Ronald Frankau, whose two records were entitled 'Oh you Ladies in the Forces' and 'The Jap, the Wop and the Hun'! Somewhat less xenophobic was Noel Coward's 'Don't let's be beastly to the Germans'. Other favourites bringing out records included Hutch with 'Hold Back the Dawn', and Dorothy Summers – alias ITMA's Mrs Mopp – who released a record that was inevitably entitled 'Can I do yer now sir?'. Popular songs that Christmas included 'Coming in on a Wing and a Prayer', 'The Homecoming Waltz', 'Besame Mucho', and of course Vera Lynn with 'There's a Ship Rolling Home'.

Pantomimes could be seen everywhere, from the children's show in the local village hall, through the repertory theatre in a small town, to the large theatres of London's West End. A taste of what was involved in a big production can be gained from the reviews; this is from that year's London Coliseum production of *Humpty Dumpty*:

Nothing has been left out. There is a room to be papered by Nervo and Knox, Naughton and Gold [all members of the Crazy Gang], and Mr Hal Bryan, and there is another room full of greenish ghouls to frighten them almost to death. There is a journey to Snowland, splendid vistas opening into vistas more splendid at journey's end, where a palace of sugar appears. There is a spirited principal boy in Miss Pat Kirkwood, and Miss Norma Dawn is there to justify the sentimental ardours. There are delightful interludes by the Ganjou Brothers, who hurl Juanita here, there, and everywhere as though she were a little feathered silver arrow. Rovi Pavinoff, that dazzling pirouettist, and the Betty Hobbs girls, who circumnavigate the stage on rolling spheres!

Other large London shows that year included *Cinderella* at His Majesty's Theatre, with Tessie O'Shea, *Alice in Wonderland* at the Scala, with Dame

HERE'S LUCK TO YAH!

In one of their rare moments of seriousness, the Crazy Gang got together,
sat down, and penned these greetings to readers of "Film Pictorial"
Christmas Annual.

The Crazy Gang, a popular British comedy troup, made up of three double acts, Bud Flanagan and Chesney Allen (back), Jimmy Nervo and Teddy Knox (centre), and Charlie Naughton and Jimmy Gold (front). Together, or in parts, they starred in many pantomimes, stage and radio shows. (*Film Pictorial*)

Sybil Thorndike as the Queen of Hearts, and Glynis John as *Peter Pan* at the Cambridge Theatre. Of course, it was not only in the capital that audiences had a wide choice. In Glasgow that year you could pick from *Puss in Boots* at the Metropolitan, *Red Riding Hood* at the Alhambra, or *Robinson Crusoe* at the Pavilion; in Leeds there was *Aladdin* at the Grand or *Cinderella* at the Royal; while in Liverpool there was a choice of *Sleeping Beauty* at the

Empire, *Mother Goose* at the Pavilion, or *Babes in the Wood* at the Royal Court. In Edinburgh you could choose from *Dick Whittington* at the Royal and *Goldilocks and the Three Bears* at the King's, while in Newcastle there was *Cinderella* at the Royal or *Babes in the Wood* at the Empire.

At the cinema, Anna Sten and Philip Dorn starred in *Chetniks*, described as 'a very moving picture of Jugoslavian patriots'. Cheryl Walker and William Terry provided the love interest in *Stage Door Canteen*, which also featured Gracie Fields. She was also starring in another new release, *Holy Matrimony*, which was not, as you might expect, a musical but rather a straight drama with Monty Wooley as her husband. *The Cross of Lorraine* had an all-male cast including Gene Kelly, Peter Lorre and Sir Cedric Hardwicke. Other US releases included *Jane Eyre* with Joan Fontaine and Orson Welles, and *For Whom the Bell Tolls* starring Gary Cooper and Ingrid Bergman, which was billed as 'The Greatest Love Story of Our Time'. British films included *Yellow Canary*, starring Anna Neagle, Richard Greene and Nova Pilbeam, in which Neagle pretends to be a Nazi sympathiser to flush out fifth columnists, and *The Lamp Still Burns*, which illustrated the trials of wartime nursing and starred Rosamund John and Stewart Granger.

The newsreels featured Winston Churchill in uniform, reviewing troops in Egypt and posing for photographs with Roosevelt and the Turkish President Ismet Inönü, while another newsreel showed British troops shopping in the market in Cairo. Ministry of Information shorts included *The Skeleton in the Cupboard*, an animated film showing the adventures of a skeleton who tries to join the army; rejected, he goes to the cinema where he sees a film showing how salvaged bones can be used, so he throws himself into a bucket marked 'bones'. Another MoI short, *The Sacred Flame*, showed Sherlock Holmes discovering the tricks by which coal could be used economically, culminating in the final message 'Save Fuel'.

That Christmas Day 17,000 people watched Liverpool beat Tranmere Rovers 2–1, and over 16,600 saw Tottenham Hotspurs beat Fulham 2–0. That day Blackpool won the North League championship for the third year running, while Rangers beat Falkirk 3–1 in the North-Eastern League Cup Final. On Boxing Day 440,000 watched the opening Football War Cup and League South games, including 13,186 who went to see Bradford Park Avenue beat Leeds 2–1, while over 20,000 watched Liverpool beating Wrexham 4–0. A Dominions Rugby Union XV, made up entirely of members of the Australian and New Zealand armed forces stationed in Britain, beat London at Richmond by 13 points to 9. There was no horse-racing but there was the usual crop of greyhound meetings.

PARTIES

Parties ranged from small family get-togethers through works parties and local dances. All sorts of local groups held Christmas parties, which were often masterpieces of improvisation. *Motor Cycling* magazine reported that: 'Once again the combined Christmas party of the Sunbeam and West Middlesex Amateur Clubs was a great success. The venue was Pimm's, near Ludgate Circus, and nearly a hundred enthusiasts turned up, some of them after travelling considerable distances. A first rate lunch was followed by a fun fair, which was later transformed into a cinema. Altogether a grand show.' The 'Club News' page proves that such seasonal get-togethers were common, although the venues

If you had the coupons, you might get a new dress for Christmas, such as this utility number from Selfridges.

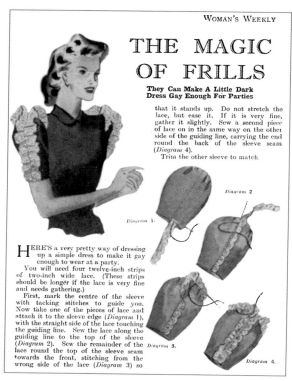

WOMAN'S WEEKLY

THE MAGIC OF FRILLS

They Can Make A Little Dark Dress Gay Enough For Parties

that it stands up. Do not stretch the lace, but ease it. If it is very fine, gather it slightly. Sew a second piece of lace on in the same way on the other side of the guiding line, carrying the end round the back of the sleeve seam (*Diagram* 4).

Trim the other sleeve to match.

Diagram 2

Diagram 1.

HERE'S a very pretty way of dressing up a simple dress to make it gay enough to wear at a party.

You will need four twelve-inch strips of two-inch wide lace. (These strips should be longer if the lace is very fine and needs gathering.)

First, mark the centre of the sleeve with tacking stitches to guide you. Now take one of the pieces of lace and attach it to the sleeve edge (*Diagram* 1), with the straight side of the lace touching the guiding line to the top of the sleeve (*Diagram* 2). Sew the lace along the guiding line to the top of the sleeve (*Diagram* 2). Sew the remainder of the *Diagram 3.* lace round the top of the sleeve seam towards the front, stitching from the wrong side of the lace (*Diagram* 3) so

Diagram 4.

For many, party frocks were now 'Make do and Mend' affairs, and women's magazines gave many ideas how to liven up an old dress.

tended to be more mundane: the Greenwich Motor-Cycle Club (MCC) met at the Prince of Orange public house, the Chelmsford & District MCC at the Horse and Groom, Ditton's MCC at the King's Arms, Reading MCC at The Crown, and so on.

People worked hard to decorate the party room, to create the right atmosphere. Stephen Spender, who like many other artists and writers had become an Auxiliary Fireman, described in 'Christmas Day at Station XIY' how crews prepared their station for their Christmas party:

First of all they blocked up all the windows of the already dark and fairly airless recreation hut. They then procured reams of crinkly paper – some of it a dark olive-green colour, the rest in bright blue – and yards of paper ribboning. They covered the walls with the dark green paper, except for the window spaces, which they covered with the blue. Then they made a lattice-work of paper ribboning on the green part of the walls by drawing the ribbons, twisted, diagonally across the wall from floor to ceiling, cross-wise. They then filled the blue spaces of the windows with a silver crescent moon and a few stars. In front of this, they superimposed curtains of yellow tissue paper.

Next they moved the stove, which was by the door, right to the back end of the room, and they painted it all over with bright silver paint. Then they built a bar by the door where the stove had been. The front

Who is this stranger dressed as Father Christmas? Why, it's Jane from the *Daily Mirror*,
losing her clothes as usual.

of this was also festooned with trellis-work of paper ribbons. Next they procured hundreds of little 'fairy' bulbs which were hidden amongst the paper festoons suspended from the ceiling.

On Christmas Eve Pickel's wife appeared with a present for the station Christmas party. It was a final master-piece, a board with 'A Merry Christmas to All' inscribed on it in flourishing, cursive script, surrounded with scrolls of glittering, powdered silver and green holly leaves.

MAKE 'PLUM DELIGHTS' FOR YOUR PARTY!

Ingredients: 1 bottle of plums, 1¾oz Brown & Poulson cornflour, 3 tablespoons water, stale cake crumbs

Stew fruit with sugar as required. When soft, rub all through sieve. Measure quantity and make it up to 1 pint with water. Put into pan to heat. Mix cornflour with the water; add to puree, stir till boiling, boil 3 minutes, stirring well. Remove from the heat, beat vigorously for a few minutes. A little orange or lemon cordial will improve the flavour. Put some stale cake crumbs into the bottom of sundae glasses, pour mixture over, leave to set. Then, decorate as liked. A few blanched plum kernels, or sifted cake crumbs, make an effective decoration.

Brown & Poulson advertisement

Wendy Peters recalled:

We used to spend time with my aunt and uncle and cousin at their wonderful house in East Morton, near Bingley, where they had an enormous Christmas tree in the ballroom, and invited children from the village to a party. I remember Christmas 1944 there. I was three years old; the tree impressed me greatly, it actually touched the ceiling. I remember sitting on a footstool and being absolutely fascinated, especially when Father Christmas, a most imposing figure, actually my uncle, came into the room with a sack of gifts for the children.

Music was important, and might be provided by the wireless or the gramophone. That Christmas Columbia and Parlophone offered Paul Jones medleys by Jack Leon and His Dance Orchestra and the Debroy Somers Band. Best of all was live music. Margaret Cushion described one party: 'We had plenty of entertainment; one of our neighbours wheeled their piano over, and we had a friend who was a busker with his accordion

A 'Paul Jones' is the very thing to 'loosen up' a party and get people acquainted

A Paul Jones, an illustration from the *Columbia Record Guide*, December 1943. Military uniforms were then part of everyday life.

and someone with a banjo, so we had a real knees-up.' Anyone who could play an instrument found themselves in great demand. Roy Burnham, who played the banjo, wrote that people would say to him: 'You must come to our party next week. It'll be great.' He used to go, 'not so much for the gay time or the free drinks,' but because, in a phrase worthy of George Formby himself, he 'never tires of showing off my banjo'.

A letter in *Picture Post* that month carried a letter entitled 'Christmas – by an American':

> It is my first Christmas in England, and I have been to my first Christmas party. Our host was a Royal Ordnance Factory in the Midlands; our hostesses the women war workers. Among the invited guests were over 1,000 children [aged] from 5 to 14. . . . To an American, the sight of the youngsters drinking gallons of tea was impressive. . . . I thought of all the American mothers who firmly believe that tea would make their children nervous wrecks! (They would probably serve up, instead, cocoa with ice-cream and cake if this could be managed on wartime rations.)

In Britain, of course, this most certainly could not have been managed.

Eric Stevens recalled: 'My other memories were of works' Christmas parties where the food was always the same – fish paste sandwiches (I hated them) and jelly.' Dorothy Adcock remembers: 'Jam and paste sandwiches was the party food on offer.'

There were many other Americans in Britain. W.J. Wheatley remembers: 'About this time thousands of American troops were arriving in the West Country to train for Operation Overlord [the D-Day invasion]. Many families round about took some of these GIs into their homes to spend Christmas Day with them. The GIs were lovely lads, only kids, some not much older than me, they were friendly, polite, and generous.' Sybil Morley remembers US airmen from Wormington air base at the rectory in Fordham:

A Christmas party for Deptford children, December 1943, partly paid for by donations from Canadian children. Notice how genuinely pleased they seem with the apples they are being given. The woman in uniform is an air-raid Warden – many Civil Defence groups laid on parties for local children or needy groups. (*Lewisham Local Studies*)

There were over 2,000 Americans there. My father made himself known to the chaplain and an invitation was given to the men to visit whenever they were able. We always seemed to have American airmen at our home, and my sister and I were very thrilled to be given a ride in their jeep when they came to collect greenery for Christmas decorations. Naturally they came on Christmas Day when we always had a party for them. They provided the ingredients for my mother to make cakes, etc.

We had sing-songs and played silly games. I always remember thinking how strange it was that these airmen could bring themselves down to the level of playing 'hide the thimble' and thoroughly enjoying themselves! They were great fun and we all had a lovely time, and they were appreciative of being invited into an English home while they were so far away from home. Of course, they always got moved on to other camps, and there were many changes, many new faces, so it was always good to meet them all. We probably had other gifts, but all I can remember was the chocolate bars and fruit and wonderful ice-cream!

One Colchester newspaper reported a typical Christmas party:

Christmas came to an American aerodrome on Saturday, December 23 [1944] when 347 children from the Colchester area visited the Eighth Air Force fighter station to be guests of the men at a Christmas party. . . . The children were from rural communities near this station. They were chaperoned by clergy of the parishes in this vicinity. The party was held in the American Red Cross Aero Club at the airfield, and started off with a series of games. Then came the high-spot of the afternoon for the youngsters – ice-cream and cake.

The 300-odd children were then taken to the post theatre, where they were shown films of 'Popeye', 'Mickey Mouse' and other cartoon characters. After the show they returned to the Aero Club and received Christmas presents from a groundcrew man, who played Santa Claus for the party complete with white wig, beard and red clothing. The room where the party was held was decorated in the Christmas spirit. A large Christmas tree stood in a corner of the room, which is used as a snack-bar in the evenings by men of this base.

The children brought a bit of home atmosphere into Christmas time for the Americans. By inviting the English children to the party, the Americans tried to repay in part the kindnesses shown them by English people in the vicinity. The men of this base contributed gifts from packages they received from home to make the children's Christmas happier.

Little eight-year-old David Cope of Fordham, whose brother Ted is with the British Army overseas, said as he was leaving for home in a GI truck, 'Gosh, I had a good time. And that ice cream!'

Christmas 1944 cover of the *Land Girl*, magazine of the Women's Land Army.

SIX

1944

The Last Wartime Christmas

The Archbishop of York's Christmas message in December 1944 was in positive vein:

> This is the sixth Christmas of the war. But it will be happier for most of us than the preceding five. The danger of invasion has passed, and the worst of the air-raids are over. With quiet confidence we see the end in sight. We hope that by next Christmas some of those now absent from us will have returned to their homes. and though we know that there will be a hard struggle both in Europe and in the Far East before victory is won, we begin to plan and to look forward to a new and better world.

All over the world the allies were making progress. On 1 December Crete had been liberated. Russian forces were advancing into Hungary, reaching the Yugoslavian border on the 7th and Czechoslovakia on the 18th. In the Far East Chinese troops on the mainland and British forces in Burma were making headway against the Japanese, while on the 19th and again on the 27th Saipan-based USAAF Super-Fortresses bombed Tokyo. On the 15th, US forces entered Germany itself – the end in the West felt tantalisingly close – but on the following day the Germans strongly counter-attacked on a 50-mile front in the Ardennes, supported by the *Luftwaffe*. Untried US troops gave way and, in a worrying repeat of 1940, German armour pushed through at an alarming rate. By Christmas Eve enemy troops had penetrated a distance of some 59 miles into Belgium.

Despite the archbishop's message of hope, this was probably the most joyless Christmas of the war on the home front. W.J. Wheatley recalled:

> 1944 was a strange Christmas. After the success of the invasion and the advance through France, you would have thought the mood would have been cock-a-hoop, but it was not. We had grim news just before Christmas of the German breakthrough in the Ardennes. People were very shaken and worried by this and also the V1s and V2s were still hitting London and the Home Counties. Many had thought the war would be over by this Christmas, but it still dragged on. The defeat at Arnhem in September set the mood for the rest of the year. I believe it was the most gloomy Christmas of the war, and bad weather did not help. The nation was weary.

Less than 2,000 tons of bombs had been dropped on Britain over the course of the year, but in June the German assault on Britain had been resumed with V-weapons, which continued the attack throughout December. The following is a description by Mrs Robert Henrey of the damage wrought on Selfridges, in London's Oxford Street, when a V2 landed next to it in the first week in December:

> I had claimed that so far there was no outward sign of Christmas, but I had not visited Selfridge's, in which case I would undoubtedly have been able to write about the fir trees illuminated with coloured globes and decorated with gay parcels which stood in every window along the whole length of the building from Orchard Street to Duke Street.
>
> These must have made a very pleasant sight and charmed the shoppers who daily surge along this famous thoroughfare. But now these poor little trees, with the ornaments torn from them, lay amongst the broken glass on the pavement, and some of them were being swept into the gutter. Such a dismal picture would have needed the genius of Hans Anderson to commit it to paper, for what can be more pathetic than a garlanded tree that comes to a tragic end two and a half weeks before Christmas Day?

The V-weapon assault drove many back to the shelters that Christmas. Kings Cross was one of the three best decorated underground station canteens that year. (*London Transport Museum*)

From the beginning of December at least 100 V2s had landed on Britain; on the 23rd they struck at Bexley, Hackney, Shoeburyness, Mildenhall and Wanstead. Eastwood and Epping were hit on Christmas Eve, the Epping rocket landing at 11.23 p.m. that evening. Also on Christmas Eve 50 Heinkel aircraft, each carrying a 'doodlebug', crossed the coast between Skegness and Mablethorpe, launching their V1s towards Manchester. Air-launched V1s were far less accurate than those launched from ramps; 19 crashed immediately or vanished, while others went wildly astray. One crashed in the Humber and one in County Durham. Most of the rest plunged to the earth in an area bounded by Leeds, Preston, Chester and Sheffield. The worst incident was at Oldham where 32 people were killed and 49 badly injured.

A Strube cartoon from early December. With the war going well, the Government promised home leave for Christmas. However, on the 16th the German counter-attack took place in the Ardennes, and a great deal of leave was cancelled.

There was a break from the bombardment on Christmas Day but they started again on Boxing Day, the first landing on Nazeing just after 9 p.m. that night. Twenty minutes later the seasonal celebrations at the crowded Prince of Wales pub in Mackenzie Road, Islington, were brutally cut short when a V2 landed there, killing 68 people.

By Christmas the V-weapons had killed nearly 8,500 British civilians. The threat from German conventional aircraft had by this time all but passed, and with it went the need for the blackout, which made no difference to the unmanned V-weapons. Consequently that Christmas, inland churches were allowed to light up their stained-glass windows for the first time since the outbreak of war.

Also irrelevant now was the Home Guard. On 3 December 7,000 members had marched through London in a final parade to mark their disbanding. The King himself took the salute. By now 4½ million men and 420,000 women were in the services, while almost 180,000 British servicemen had fallen into the bag.

It was a cold, foggy December in Britain. With the end of raids by the *Luftwaffe* the restrictions on reporting the weather had been relaxed. *The Times* announced: 'Throughout the [Christmas] day the thermometer at Air Ministry meteorological stations at Kew, Boscombe Down, Bristol, Birmingham, Mildenhall, Cranwell, and Manchester did not rise above freezing point. The coldest county was Lincolnshire, where there was never less than 5 degrees of frost. Fog persisted in most places.' Mrs Robert Henrey wrote:

Christmas Day was white – not with snow, but with hoar-frost that lay like a thick carpet over the parks. The temperature, below zero, contracted the muscles of one's face, and froze the puddles on the gravel walks. The sump, facing the Cornish Elms in the Green Park drawing room, had a coating of ice, and the roofs of the black huts studded round the big searchlight looked as if somebody had decorated them with sugar-icing. A crimson sun, low in the sky in the direction of Victoria, was trying hard to penetrate the white mist that shrouded the wintry scene.

The Ministry of Food announced treats for the Christmas period: an extra ½lb of sugar, ½lb of margarine, meat up from 1*s* 2*d* to 1*s* 10*d* (or an extra 6oz of cheese for vegetarians) and ½lb of sweets for holders of children's or junior ration books. The over-seventies were also given an additional ounce of tea each. Interestingly, the extra meat ration had to be taken between 17 and 23 December, except in Scotland, where it had to be taken between the 24th and the 30th. *Woman* magazine commented: 'Just a little more sugar and a little more fat – but how much more is it when it comes to making a few small luxuries for Christmas. One of the nicest presents to give (or to receive) is a half-pound of homemade sweets, and we are lucky enough now to be able to spare a little raw material for sweet-making. If you make sweets for presents, try to collect some transparent wrapping paper to make them into gay little packets for giving.' The article then gave recipes for toffee apples, humbugs, caramel fudge, lemon barley sugar, peppermint creams, buttered nuts, and Russian jellies.

One suggestion for presents was 'marzipan fruits'. These were rolled into the shape of apples, pears and so on, and coloured with food colouring, with cloves used as stalks and their heads pressed in to form the dried flower head. Arranged in a basket, readers were assured, they would make a fine gift.

Despite the fact that shipping losses during the previous year had plummeted to 1 million tons, the shortages were biting deeper than ever. Wendy Peters recalled:

Somehow my mother and aunt had managed to get their hands on some dried fruit. Mint and currant pasty was such a delicacy in Yorkshire. It had been sorely missed during the war, so imagine the great performance when they baked one and took it from the oven – oh, the aroma! The pasty was left on the kitchen table to cool; later, when my mother and aunt went back into the kitchen, they discovered my aunt's rather large cat perched on top of it, enjoying the warmth. Needless to say the pasty was given a hasty dusting down, and nothing was said, as the rest of the family devoured the pasty with a relish that only years of deprivation could induce.

SHORT CRUST PASTRY

Make a short crust pastry of 8oz self-raising flour and 2oz lard or cooking fat. Roll out. Divide into two and line a tart tin with the smaller half. Sprinkle with 2 tablespoons finely chopped mint. Spread with 6 heaped tablespoons cooked and grated carrot, mixed with 2oz sugar and three or four drops of lemon substitute. Cover with another 2 tablespoons mint. Cover with the remaining pastry, seal edges, make a hole in the centre. Bake in a brisk oven. Cut into squares, serve cold.

The Kitchen Front gave a recipe for wartime mint pasty, using carrot instead of currants (some people substituted elderberries).

The following recipes, though rather long, give a great insight into the extent of shortages by this time – and illustrate the resourcefulness of the recipe writers at the Stork Margarine Cookery Service!

Christmas Trifle (serves 12)

Bottom Layer: 1lb apples, fresh or bottled (or any other fruit), 1 tablespoonful sugar or syrup, a few drops of almond essence (if liked), 1 tablespoonful water.

If bottled fruit is used, drain off liquid. Cook the fruit gently with the sugar and 1 tablespoonful water (if liked, add a few drops of almond essence), and spread evenly in the bottom of a large glass bowl.

Sponge: 2 level tablespoonsful dried egg, 2 tablespoonsful sugar, 5 tablespoonsful warm water, 3oz self-raising flour, pinch of salt, 1 teaspoonful baking powder, 2 tablespoonsful jam for filling, 2 heaped tablespoonsful dried household milk.

NOTE: this recipe can only be made successfully with dry household milk and it is important that the mixture is beaten exactly as instructed.

Sieve the dried egg and milk powder into a medium-sized mixing bowl or mix with the fingers, rubbing out the lumps. Add 3 tablespoonsful warm water and mix to a smooth paste, beating well. Add the remaining 2 tablespoonsful warm water, a tablespoonful at a time, and beat in smoothly. Add the sugar and beat briskly and rapidly with a wire whisk for 15 minutes. Sieve the flour, salt and baking powder together and fold in quickly with a metal spoon. Turn into a well-greased sandwich tin (6.5–7 inches across) and bake for 20 minutes on the middle shelf of a moderately hot oven (Regulo Mark 5). Cool, cut open, spread with jam, put together again and cut into 8 portions. Place on top of the apples in the dish, pressing well down.

Jam Sauce: 2 tablespoonsful jam, ¼ pint water or homemade wine or syrup from sweetened bottled fruit. Put the jam and the water in a saucepan and bring to the boil, stirring well. Cool slightly and pour evenly over the sponge. Leave to soak for about half an hour.

Custard: 1 pint milk (fresh or household), 2 teaspoonsful sugar, 1oz custard powder, or 2 level tablespoonsful each of dried egg and flour and half a teaspoonful of vanilla.

If custard powder is used, mix to a smooth paste with a little of the cold milk. Bring the remainder of the milk to the boil, add the sugar and pour over the mixed custard powder, stirring all the time. Cool slightly and pour over the sponge.

If made with flour and egg, mix together the flour, dried egg and sugar, add a little milk and mix to a smooth paste. Gradually add the remainder of the cold milk, put in a saucepan and bring to the boil over a gentle heat, stirring all the time, until the mixture thickens. Cook for a further 3 minutes, add the vanilla, cool slightly and pour over the sponge. Allow the custard to become completely cold before putting on the cream.

Cream for Topping: Quarter pint of milk (fresh or household), 1 level dessertspoonful cornflour, or 1 level tablespoonful flour, 1 heaped or 1 level desertspoonful sugar, 1oz margarine.

Blend the cornflour or flour smoothly with a little of the cold milk. Bring the rest of the milk to the boil and pour over the blended cornflour, stirring all the time. Return to the saucepan and cook for 3 minutes, stirring continuously. Pour the mixture into a basin and leave until quite cold. Cream the margarine and sugar together and beat in the cornflour mixture very gradually, using a wooden spoon or a wire whisk and beating well, so that the mixture becomes light and fluffy. Spread the cream evenly over the top of the trifle, then run a fork lightly all over the surface to give a ridged effect.

Decorations: Bottled cherries, or whole bottled plums cut in squares. Bottled cherries are very good for this purpose. Dry them well before using, otherwise the juice will discolour the cream. Place one in the centre and arrange the others in two circles round it, or in any other pattern desired.

Battenberg Cake

This is a wartime version of the delicious pre-war two-colour sponge cake covered with almond paste. In our recipe we use pastry instead of the latter.

Measure into two portions the following ingredients: 8oz self-raising flour, 3 reconstituted dried eggs, 3oz margarine, quarter teaspoonful salt, 3 tablespoonsful sugar, 3 tablespoonsful milk. Other ingredients required: Pink colouring, Jam for filling, vanilla or any other flavouring desired. This cake is made from two batters; when baked, each should be about 4 inches by 8 inches. Use an oblong or square tin, divided into 2 sections each this size by pieces of cardboard. Line the sections with greaseproof paper brushed with melted margarine.

For the plain portion, cream the margarine and sugar together and beat in the egg alternately with a little of the flour (sieved with the salt). Add the remainder of the flour with the milk and flavouring and fold in. Spread evenly in one partition of the tin.

Proceed as for above with the coloured portion, beating in the colouring after all the egg has been added. Spread evenly in the other partition. Bake for 25–30 minutes on the second shelf of a moderately hot oven (Regulo Mark 5).

When cold, trim off the edges of both slabs of cake and even the top. Put one portion on top of the other and cut down the centre lengthwise and across to make 8 pieces of the same size. Now join the white portion to the pink portion with jam. Spread the top lightly with jam, join two more portions together and press down lightly on top of the other slab so that the white is on top of the pink and vice versa. Continue until all the portions have been used, then trim the sides and ends so that the cake forms a perfect oblong.

NOTE: the scraps of cake that have been cut off can be used for cake crumbs for puddings, trifles, etc.

Pastry for Coating: 2oz self-raising flour, ¾oz margarine, three-quarters of a tablespoonful of dried egg mixed with 1½ tablespoonsful water. Cream the margarine, beat in the egg alternately with a little of the flour. Work in the remainder of the flour, knead lightly on a floured board, roll out very thinly into a strip wide enough to go round the cake. Place the cake on top and trim off the edges of the pastry evenly with the edge of the cake. Fold the pastry over to make sure that it is long enough to cover the cake and overlap the join. Fold back again and trim the ends. Brush the sides of the cake with jam and one end of the pastry with water. Then fold over, pressing gently down round the sides, and seal the two ends smoothly. Flute the edges along the top and mark in lines with the back of a knife. Place on a baking sheet and bake for fifteen minutes, in a fairly hot oven (Regulo Mark 6).

DECEMBER 16, 1944

CECILE'S COOKERY CLASS

The CAKE
For
Xmas Day

**It Has Wartime Ingredients
But The Same Good Old-
Fashioned Festive Air**

TO MAKE THE CAKE

3 ounces of sugar. ¼ lb. of fat
1 tablespoonful of golden syrup. ¾ lb. of fruit
3 level tablespoonfuls of dried egg
6 tablespoonfuls of water. ½ lb. of flour
¼ level teaspoonful of bi-carbonate soda
1 level teaspoonful of mixed spice
1 level teaspoonful of ground ginger

SIFT the flour with the soda and spices, and clean and prepare the fruit.
    Beat the sugar and fat to a soft cream. Sift the dried
egg and mix it to a smooth paste with half the water, then
stir in the remainder. Beat this into the creamed fat and
sugar, one-third of it at a time, stirring the mixture quickly
between each addition, then beat in the golden syrup.
    Stir in half the flour gradually, then mix the remainder
with the prepared fruit and add gradually.
    Mix all these ingredients together, and if any more moisture
is required, add a dessertspoonful of milk, then turn the
mixture into a greased cake tin, and partially hollow out
the mixture from the centre. Put the cake into a very
moderate oven to bake, reducing the heat when the cake
has risen and is beginning to brown. About one hour and a
half to one hour and three-quarters should be sufficient
time to allow.
    Test the cake with a skewer before removing it from the
oven, and when it is cooked let it stand a while before turning
it out of the tin.

VARIATION.—*The fruit
may be increased to 1 lb.
and another egg added.
The cake will then take
a little longer to bake,
probably two hours.*

TO MAKE THE ICING

¼ lb. of sugar. 4 dessertspoonfuls of water
2¼ ounces of margarine. ¼ lb. of soya flour
Vanilla or almond flavouring essence
Jam to spread on the cake

PUT the margarine into a saucepan with the water and
three-fourths of the sugar. Warm slowly until the
margarine is melted, then stir in the soya flour, and add
flavouring essence to taste.
    Sprinkle the remainder of the sugar on the pastry-board,
turn the paste on to it and work in the sugar. Pat and roll
the paste into a round to fit the top of the cake, sprinkling a
little more sugar on the board if the paste sticks.
    Spread a little jam on the top of the cake and mould the
paste on to it, making it as level as possible. If the cake is
not level, either cut it level, or level it with a small piece of
the paste before covering the whole top. The paste may be
given a slightly rough finish if preferred. Trim the edge
and mark it with a fork, then leave it to dry and decorate
the top of the cake with Christmas novelties.

If you could find the ingredients for a cake, and especially the icing, it would be at best
partly covered, as with this example from *Woman's Weekly*.

For those who could not get a chicken or a turkey, the Ministry of Food came up with a recipe for 'Braised Stuffed Veal Bird', made from 2–3 pounds of fillet or breast of veal. It could also be made with breast of lamb, beef, steak or pork, and required an ounce of fat for frying and a pound of mixed root vegetables (not potatoes). The meat was flattened, rolled and tied, then braised in stock or water with the vegetables, then it was stuffed and served up with potatoes and sprouts.

Strangely enough, despite being given this recipe, people still hunted for turkeys. Georgina Foord remembers:

A week before Christmas 1944. Rationing had its iron grip round the nation's shopping basket. I was 3 years old at the time but clearly remember the excitement when Dad said he had met a man in the pub who could get us a turkey for Christmas!

So on Christmas Eve off he went with Mum's shopping bag – and eventually arrived home with the turkey – following behind him on a piece of string. His benefactor had failed to say the turkey would be far from oven-ready! Needless to say, the turkey spent a comfortable couple of days in the garden shed, and Mum worked a bit of magic with the family's corned beef ration.

STUFFING

Wash and grate three large carrots, mix with two teacups of breadcrumbs, 3oz chopped suet or margarine, one teaspoon of sultanas, a pinch of grated nutmeg, a pinch of ginger and one tablespoonful of dried egg. When well mixed, add just enough milk and water to bind. Use as a stuffing for turkey, goose or chicken.

Woman magazine offered a tasty recipe for stuffing:

Not to be outdone, the Ministry of Food offered 'Orange Flavoured Whip':

The Ministry of Food also gave other suggestions for party food 'which will make your party remembered with delight by guests and hostess alike'. Alcoholic drinks

ORANGE FLAVOURED WHIP

1lb stewed or bottled plums, 2½ level tablespoons dried milk (dry), 3 level tablespoons of the new sweet marmalade. Strain the plums and keep the juice for a sauce or jelly. Mash the plums and mix with the milk and marmalade. Beat well. Serve in individual dishes topped with marmalade or custard. Other delicious combinations are apples and plum jam; rhubarb and raspberry jam – and you can think of many others. These fruit whips are very easy to make and great favourites at children's parties.

It's in the air—the aroma of the Christmas dinner! With lots of thick brown gravy made with Bisto. In peacetime or wartime, no meat dish is complete without **BISTO**.

The Ministry of Food recipe writers were working overtime to come up with fresh ideas. Bisto, on the other hand, still harped back to the bird that few would enjoy that year.

Let us help with YOUR PARTY

Somebody's coming home on leave. It's somebody's birthday. Or just a little party for the children. And it makes a break. But don't let the preparation for it break *you*. Here are some suggestions, sweet and savoury, which will make your party remembered with delight by guests and hostess alike.

FORK AND FINGER SAVOURIES

Sandwiches immediately suggest themselves, but to save cutting so many slices of bread, why not have some of those open "spreads"? They look so tempting and colourful. *First — the bases.* It's nice to have a variety, and there are many to choose from : national bread, brown bread, rolls, "crispbread," squares or cases of pastry.

Some Hints for the Spreads :

 1. Thin neat slices of cold meat or canned meat, decorated with strips of beetroot arranged like the spokes of a wheel or with latticed lines of finely grated raw carrot.

2. A layer of curried white fish or canned salmon, decorated with lines of chopped hard-boiled egg.

3. A round of hard-boiled egg (made with dried eggs), a slightly smaller round of beetroot on top, a pinch of parsley in the middle.

4. Grated cheese, well seasoned, mixed with a little salad dressing and criss-crossed with strips of celery.

And here are some other ideas :

EGG BOATS. Split some small rolls, scoop out some of the crumb, and spread the hollow with a little meat extract or vegetable extract or chutney; fill with scrambled egg mixed with a little white sauce.

CELERY BASKETS. Cut a few sticks of tender, crisp celery into 3-inch lengths. Fill with a mixture of mashed potato and grated cheese and colour a nice pink with bottled tomato pulp. Sprinkle a pinch of finely chopped parsley on top.

LITTLE MEAT BALLS. Mix equal quantities of chopped canned meat or cold meat and breadcrumbs and a little chopped cooked onion if you have it.

Season, and bind with reconstituted dried eggs. Roll into balls the size of walnuts, egg and breadcrumb them (reconstituted dried egg again), and fry. Delicious hot or cold.

INDIVIDUAL SALADS. Pretty as flowers and so refreshing ! Shred finely the heart of a cabbage and toss in a little salad dressing. Arrange on small glass plates if possible; decorate with grated carrot, diced beetroot and a sprinkling of chopped dried egg or grated cheese.

FOR THE CHILDREN'S PARTY

LOLLIPOP CUSTARDS. Make a thick custard in the usual way with dried eggs and household milk or fresh milk. Flavour if liked with almond, vanilla or other cooking flavour. Pour into individual glasses. Sprinkle with crushed "boiled sweets" — the more mixed the colours the better. Top with a marsh-mallow, piece of turkish delight, square of fudge or other soft sweet.

FRUITY BUNS. Chopped apple, mixed with dried fruit — raisins, sultanas or chopped prunes — bound with jam and sandwiched between halves of buns.

ORANGE TRIFLE. Sponge sandwich — you can make lovely light ones with dried eggs — spread liberally with sweet orange marmalade. Saturate with orange squash diluted and sweetened to taste. Top with custard, decorate with mock cream and grated chocolate.

FREE LEAFLET—"Festive Fare" containing many other recipes and suggestions gladly sent free on receipt of a postcard. Please mention this leaflet by name, and address The Ministry of Food, Food Advice Division, London, W.I. (S109).

ISSUED BY THE MINISTRY OF FOOD

American soldiers and Red Cross nurses watch British children opening their Christmas presents. (*Associated Press*)

Finding your favourite prewar Christmas tipple had become a matter of some detective work, as this advert for VP Rich Ruby sherry implies.

were now harder to obtain than ever: 'Among the half million inhabitants of Kensington, Hammersmith, Fulham and Chelsea, only one woman was arrested for drunkenness over the holiday (she was fined 2*s* 6*d*).' However, the Victoria Stores (full free off-licence) in London's Victoria advertised: 'Christmas Spirit – In spite of the shortage of Wines and Spirits this Christmas we are able to offer a full selection of the following; fine old brandy (3 star), Jamaica rum, selected port (type) wine, pale golden sherry, full rich ruby wine, full rich white wine, full strength tawny wine, ginger wine (alcoholic), matured London gin, orange gin, lemon gin, vint-egg, vermouth (sweet or dry), cocktails, [and] a few bottles of liqueurs', but as usual 'supplies are limited'.

The Times of 27 December commented: 'Throughout the country there was manifest a consciousness of the approach of the end of the European conflict. In many quarters there was apparent a desire greater than in the past war years to make holiday, and to visit distant relatives and friends. Many people left London for Scotland and the north of England, Wales and the West Country, and the south coast. On all the main lines on Saturday [23 December] there was considerable passenger traffic.' On Christmas Day itself, however, the gates of the London Underground stations were closed, as an unofficial strike by staff closed all lines. Travellers found themselves faced with a limited bus service, which ended at about 4.00 in the afternoon. Meanwhile, the Post Office reported that it had processed some 350 million items of Christmas post.

Shortages were, by now, acute. In Bury, John Fletcher had continued to operate the fund which he had started in 1940, to provide Christmas presents for the Channel Islands' evacuee children in the town, but this year he was forced to stop, not because of lack of funding but because of shortages of available goods. Similarly the BBC's annual Christmas Day 'Wireless for the Blind appeal' did not take place, 'due to the lack of radio sets available'.

Jones & Higgins' store in Peckham advertised 'Useful Christmas Gifts' for sale. These give a good insight into the lack of choice and the high

All in a Day's Work
— By Rick Elmes

Conspicuous consumption was clearly identified as the province of black marketeers or profiteers, as this *Daily Herald* cartoon illustrates.

prices of whatever was available. They included pairs of wooden candlesticks, finished in light oak colour, at 12s 10d a pair, and a letter-rack made of light oak at 7s 3d. There were also leather flap-jacks (powder compacts) in various colours at 11s 5d each, and of course, for men, ties in various colours for 3s 6d to 11s 6d. More expensively, they offered 'Ladies' black seal fur-backed gauntlets, at £5 a pair plus two coupons'.

The dearth of available gifts is summed up by this advice from *Woman's Weekly*:

MATCHES

Once a small thing, a box of matches now makes a very welcome gift. If you want to make this more important-looking, dress the box up by sticking a scrap of pretty wallpaper, or decorative Christmas paper at the front and back of it. Should you have more than one box to give away, a packet of one or two, decorated differently and tied with a ribbon, makes the present something other than mere matches.

Even homemade gifts were difficult as raw materials were in short supply. *Woman* magazine suggested tea- and coffee-cosies made from brightly coloured braid. Wendy Peters wrote:

> My mother was a talented seamstress, and many of my Christmas gifts were soft toys made by her from whatever materials were available. On receiving a particularly amazing Pinocchio doll, I was heard to utter the words, 'Father Christmas may have brought him, but he's wearing Mummy's felt hat!' My father made me wonderful toys: a sweet shop with 'Wendy's Sweet & Candy Shop' in red letters on a cream façade was one Christmas thrill for me; it had shelves and was fitted out with tiny bottles of dolly mixtures, etc.

The booklet *Gifts you can make yourself* gave instructions for several presents, including a ration book case made of 'skiver skin', a crumb set made of raffia, a steam roller made from old tins, knitted fair-isle slippers, and a lapel mascot.

LAPEL MASCOT

Materials – A small quantity of odds and ends of wool.
This little mascot manikin is easily made from your odd scraps of wool. For his body wind your wool round a 4-inch piece of card. The more wool you wind the fatter he will be. Slip a short length of wool through the top and knot loosely. Repeat at the lower end of the card.

Repeat the process for the arms on a 2-inch card.

Slip the body part off the card and tie a length of wool round the middle. Slip the arms off the card and put between the two halves of the body and tie off just above for the neck. Then divide the wool at the base of the body for the legs. Tie off for the ankles, cut the loops and fray out.

Tie off the ends of the arms and at the top of the head, and cut the loops for his arms and hair. Fasten him firmly to a safety pin.

A raffia crumb set, a ration book case and a lapel mascot were some of the basic gift ideas from the book, 'Gifts You Can Make Yourself', produced that year. These give a good idea of the simplicity of most handmade gifts in this last Christmas of the war.

A BOW OF LAVENDER

A lavender bow would make such a luxurious little Christmas gift for a friend. The bow is made with picot-edged organdie ribbon, about 2½ inches wide. The 'loops' of it are cleverly filled with lavender.

Take a 16-inch length of ribbon, fold the ends towards the centre, and then oversew the sides neatly with matching Sylko. Fill these 'bag loops' with lavender and sew up the openings, gathering up the centre like a bow. Take another length of the ribbon about 10½ inches long, slope the ends, and stitch it behind the lavender-filled loops, pleating up the fullness in the middle. Make a narrow organdie band, half an inch wide and 2½ inches long, and place this round the gathered centre, to form the 'knot' of the bow and hide the gathers. Stitch the ends of the strips together neatly at the back. The bow could be filled with potpourri if preferred.

The lavender bow, from *Woman's Weekly* clearly show the paucity of materials for even homemade presents.

More than ever that year, presents sent by family members serving abroad might indeed be something to look forward to. The *Daily Express* of the 18th ran an article on newly liberated Paris: 'The soldiers come for a precious 48 hours of rest, relaxation and, above everything else just now, to do a spot of Christmas shopping.' The article went on to state that the average British serviceman was spending between £5 and £10 on presents, and somewhat meanly continued: 'If you receive a parcel from Paris with an Army postmark, these are the things which you are likely to find inside it, and the prices your son, husband, brother or boy-friend is likely to have paid, translated at the present exorbitant rate of 200 francs to the pound: Perfume: famous makes like Molyneux, Chanel and Lanvin cost about £3 for a small bottle and are becoming hard to get even at that price. There is plenty of lesser known perfume around for about £1 a bottle.' It went on to mention lipsticks at 8*s* each, rayon stockings from 12*s* to 30*s* a pair, silk scarves from £1 to £30, and fancy notepaper – 'a Paris speciality' – from 6*s* a box upwards. 'Most popular are the large decorative earrings which all Paris girls are now wearing. They can cost anything from £10 to £20 and more, but the cheap kinds, made of cloth, beads or metal, are just as festive-looking as the expensive ones. For men

– mostly pipes at £1 or so and fountain pens, which can still be got here for 3*s* 6*d*.'

Brussels, too, had become an official leave town for British troops on a 48-hour pass – this Christmas that was 12,000 troops of the Second Army every 2 days. They too could buy things unavailable in Britain. *Picture Post* of 23 December reported:

The shops are filled with toys such as English children haven't had in their lives. There's scent and cosmetics, wine, and briar pipes, wonderful fruit and lace (for which Brussels has always been famous); indeed, everything except meat, tobacco, sweets and clothes (although there are some silk stockings). The trouble is that, although Brussels has everything, every-

Cards like this one would be received by the families of many servicemen in Europe. On the back is written the poignant message: 'My Darling Iris. . . . wishing you a very happy Christmas, and the next one together, Your own Harry.'

thing in Brussels costs the earth. The price of a cup of coffee is five shillings. A doll for a soldier's daughter costs him about three weeks' pay.

A teddy-bear cost almost as much as a doll, an electric toy train would cost all of £20, and a toy jeep 7*s* 6*d*. In spite of the high cost, many of the troops did take the opportunity to buy Christmas presents, especially as servicemen were allowed to send home four parcels a year, each of £2 value, tax free.

Vera Sibley remembers how coveted these rarities were: 'Being young (I was 14 when the war started) I missed the "fol-de-rols", like make-up and pretty things to wear. My sister's husband came home on leave from Italy and brought her some face powder; sleeping in the same bedroom as her, I stole some. She smelled it on me, and I caught it in the neck for taking her stuff, but it was such a temptation, believe me.'

Gifts from abroad were not only from servicemen, as Bryan Farmer explained:

Our family was fortunate to have relations who had emigrated to South Africa after the First World War. Each year we eagerly awaited the annual Christmas gifts in the flattened and tattered package that they had posted some three months previously. We were never disappointed, despite the squashed contents. They would always send a colourful calendar with pictures of the wild animals of Africa, the beautiful sunlit beaches, stunning views of Table Mountain and of the Zulu and other black folk bedecked in their bright tribal dress. But this was always of secondary importance to the packets of crystallised fruits, bars of Cadbury's chocolate, little miniatures of banana liqueurs and suchlike; something for every one of us.

The Archbishop of York gave his annual Christmas message, part of which ran: 'From early morning to late at night on Christmas Day the wireless will carry both to those at home and to their friends and kinsfolk far away the news of God's love to mankind and His promise of peace to men of good will.' The last clause is very interesting. There had been quite a debate early in the war about the use of the traditional phrase 'Peace on Earth, good will to all men'. All men, of course, included the Germans as a whole, and more specifically Hitler and his crew, and it was widely felt that peace and goodwill were certainly not to be extended to *them*, and hence the compromise 'peace to men of good will'.

Christmas Day programmes on the Home Service included all the old favourites: orchestras, children's carols, light music, Uncle Mac, and ENSA shows. *The Journey Home* was the optimistic title of this year's reunion programme: 'As a prologue to our journey we celebrate the fact that a large part of Europe is free again, and we ask listeners to travel with us to Paris for Christmas Eve Mass in the Cathedral of Notre Dame, and to join with the People of France in their thanksgiving for liberation.' Then it was on to a party given by a detachment of the London Home Guard for children of men serving overseas, a partisans' party in Paris, then to a party given by British servicemen for children in Brussels. There followed the usual round-the-world link-up.

In his speech, the King looked to the postwar years: 'The defeat of Germany and Japan is only the first half of our task; the second is to create a world of free men "untouched by tyranny". . . . I wish you, from my heart, a happy Christmas; and, for the coming year, a full measure of that courage and faith in God which alone enables us to bear old sorrows and face new trials, until the day when the Christmas message – peace on earth and goodwill towards men – finally comes true.'

In the afternoon came Henry Hall, and *The Rose and the King*, billed as a 'fireside pantomime'. That evening's big programme was *The AEF Show*. The *Radio Times* of 22 December listed the content as the 'Second half of a two-hour broadcast from the Allied Expeditionary Forces Programme, including the American Band of the AEF directed by Major Glenn Miller'. Sadly, it was not to be. Just after 6 p.m. on Christmas Eve the BBC interrupted its broadcast to report that 'Major Glenn Miller, the well-known American band leader, is reported missing; he left England by air for Paris nine days ago.'

At 8 p.m. there was *Christmas Night at Eight*, featuring Arthur Askey, Richard 'Stinker' Murdoch and Kenneth Horne in *Christmas at Much Binding in the Marsh*, Elsie and Doris Waters, James Moody and the Bachelor Girls, Barbara Mullin, and an enlarged *Puzzle Corner*. The last big programme was *Christmas Cabaret from the Nuffield Centre, London*, with Jack Jackson and his Band, Helen Clare and Ivor Dennis, Cyril Fletcher, Dorothy Carless, Jack and Daphne Barker, and Murgatroyd and Winterbottom.

The General Forces Programme included *A Christmas Party* for children of men serving overseas, the Christmas Day Service from Southwark Cathedral, Association Football (Chelsea v. West Ham), *Christmas at St Bart's*, which was an ENSA broadcast from the London Hospital, and *Command Performance*, a show from the American Forces Network.

The latest British films included *Madonna of the Seven Moons*, with Phyllis Calvert, Stewart Granger and Patricia Roc, and the ever-popular George Formby in *He Snoops to Conquer*, supported by Robertson Hare. In a more patriotic vein there was the splendid *Henry V* with Laurence Olivier, or the Crown Film Unit's documentary-style film *Western Approaches*, about the adventures of a group of torpedoed merchant seamen adrift in a lifeboat. For those who liked American films there was *Casanova Brown*, with Gary Cooper and Frank Morgan; the classic *Double Indemnity*, with Fred McMurray, Barbara Stanwyck and Edward G. Robinson; *Hail the Conquering Hero*, starring Edie Bracken; *In Society*, with Abbott and Costello; and the less memorable *I Love a Soldier* with Paulette Goddard and Sonny Tufts. There were also the usual musicals, including *Step Lively* with the new heart-throb Frank Sinatra, *Christmas Holiday* with Deanna Durbin, Gene Kelly and Adolphe Menjou, and *Irish Eyes are Smiling* with Dick Haymes and Monty Wooley.

As usual, the newsreels showed British troops enjoying their Christmas dinner, while one depicted troops hosting a party for Dutch children; there was also an item called *Toy Cargo from the USA*, showing a large number of toys donated to the children of Britain by American children, and Father Christmas handing them out. The Ministry of Information put out a short film, *Salute to Housewives*, showing Navy and Army officers, a paratrooper and a farmer giving thanks to housewives for their efforts in collecting salvage.

Another short was a cartoon of Father Christmas. His house resembles a huge white postbox. On Christmas Eve thousands of letters and parcels come through the letter box and pile up with him sitting on top of them. His sleigh is so weighed down that it crashes into a snowdrift, out of which he pokes his head and says: 'If only people would post earlier. Remember, post before December 18th if you can.'

The theatre suffered, like everything else, from shortages, and the consequent make-do-and-mend solutions. Robina Hinton remembers this well, from personal, and rather painful, experience:

Late in the war I was playing the Dover Hippodrome. I started the act by doing big pirouettes around the stage; I got to one corner and went right through the stage – the woodworm had got to it. Luckily the audience thought it was all part of the act.

There was a shortage of musicians as men were called up; some of them were very bad. There were also shortages of stage-hands. As the war went on and costumes got harder to replace, we used to hunt Chovey [second-hand] shops for 1920s evening dresses, covered in sequins or diamante; we would then cut them down. You did get a few coupons for a new show, but very few. You could also get petrol coupons from the Showman's Guild if you had to travel to a new show, but only just enough. If you got lost, and remember there were no signposts or maps, you wouldn't have enough to get there, so if we came to a hill we used to switch the engine off and coast down it.

By now, much British music had an American feel, such as 'Got Any Gum Chum?', the question put by British children to any US serviceman they came into contact with, and the far-from-PC 'Choc'late Soldier from the USA'. Others included 'A Fellow on a Furlough', 'Jungle Jive', 'Is You is or is You ain't?', 'Spring Will be a Little Late this Year', Judy Garland's 'The Trolley Song' and, of course, 'Have Yourself a Merry Little Christmas', both the latter from the film *Meet Me in St Louis*. Some songs

Got any gum chum? was the universal question posed to US servicemen. The Yanks had brought with them such rarities as chewing gum, nylons and ice cream, and also their music – the waltz had been replaced by the jitterbug. America came to stand for everything the British couldn't get – things would never really be the same again.

naturally referred to the approaching end to hostilities, such as 'Shine on Victory Moon' and 'When we Dance at the Victory Ball'.

On Saturday 23 December the North and West Football League championships were decided, with Huddersfield Town and Cardiff City respectively coming out on top. On Christmas Day a crowd of 16,958 watched the League South leaders, Tottenham Hotspurs, beat Queens Park Rangers 4–2, but the dismal weather forced many other games to be postponed, including Bolton Wanderers v. Stockport County, Leicester City v. Nottingham Forest, Walsall v. Birmingham, Chelsea v. West Ham, and Wolverhampton Wanderers v. Stoke City. Others were abandoned, including Aston Villa v. Northampton Town, and Coventry City v. West Bromwich Albion.

Christmas Day's rugby league matches were also affected, with matches at Leeds, Castleford and Oldham postponed; on Boxing Day Hunslet v. Leeds was postponed and St Helens v. Wigan abandoned. Rugby union fared little better, with three of the six scheduled games having to be postponed. The Boxing Day football matches fared a little better; a bumper crowd of 35,226 watched Everton draw 2–2 with the old enemy Liverpool, in the Liverpool Senior Cup Final, but the opening of racing's National Hunt season, due to restart at Windsor and Wetherby that day after a lapse of nearly three years, had to be postponed after both meetings were abandoned. Several greyhound meetings did take place, however, including those at Liverpool Seaforth, Manchester White City, Newcastle White City, Newport and Slough.

Postscript

Peace at last! 1945 brought the end of the war, but not yet a return to the trappings of a peacetime Christmas. According to *The Times* on 27 December 1945:

> People made the most of their first peace-time Christmas for six years. In the words of the King, they still had to 'make a little go a long way', though the extra meat, margarine, sugar, and sweets allocated in good time ensured that a near approach to traditional fare was possible in most homes. Even oranges were obtainable once again in London and other districts.
>
> There were large congregations in church and chapel, betokening profound gratitude for the return of peace. Worshippers in St Paul's Cathedral and Westminster Cathedral had as neighbours Americans and other overseas servicemen, many of whom were spending their last Christmas in this country. American troops entertained children in clubs and halls.
>
> Otherwise, the family circle, reinforced this year by the return – in many cases after absences of five or six years – of fathers, brothers and sisters from war service, was, as in the more carefree days, the centre of Christmas celebrations.

As if to signify an end to the hard times, 'the holiday was agreeably mild, dry and green. The maximum temperature of 43° in London was 15 degrees higher than a year ago'.

Yet of course there was a sad side. The King's Christmas speech that year summed it up:

There will be the vacant places of those who will never return, brave souls who gave their all to win peace for us. We remember them with pride and with unfading love, praying that a greater peace than ours may now be theirs. There are those of you, still to be numbered in millions, who are spending a Christmas far away from your homes, engaged in east and west in the long and difficult task of restoring to shattered countries the means and manners of civilised life. But many anxieties have been lifted from you and from your folk at home: and the coming of peace brings you nearer to your heart's desire.

Those who thought victory would bring the immediate end of shortages found themselves proved woefully wrong. At Christmas 1946 George Orwell wrote in *Tribune*:

But ought we to overeat and overdrink this Christmas? We ought not to, nor will most of us get the opportunity. I am writing in praise of Christmas, but Christmas 1947, or perhaps 1948. The world as a whole is not exactly in a condition for festivities this year. . . . So I wish everyone an old-fashioned Christmas in 1947, and meanwhile, half a turkey, three tangerines, and a bottle of whisky at not more than double the legal price.

Yet things did not get better by 1947, or indeed by 1948, when Christmas was be one of the coldest on record, and coal was rationed. Arnold Beardwell recollected: 'I used to catch a train to Colchester from 1946 to 1949. Sometimes it did not turn up, and they said it was [due to] shortages of coal.' Indeed, in the postwar years rationing became more severe. Bread and potatoes were included for the first time, and it was not until 1953 that Britain at last celebrated its first postwar ration-free Christmas.

Bibliography

Books:

Bombers Over Merseyside, Liverpool Daily Echo and Post, 1943
From Brownhill to Pitch Hill, Sayers Croft Evacuation Group, *c.* 1997
Gifts You Can Make Yourself, Odhams Press, 1944
Our Blitz – Red Sky over Manchester, Kemsley Newspapers Ltd, 1943
Crompton, Richmal, *William and the Evacuees*, Newnes, 1940
Fincham, Paul, *The Home Front in the Second World War*, Longman, 1988
Haisman, M. and Snellgrove, L.E., *Dear Merv – Dear Bill*, Gomer Press, 1992
Henrey, Mrs Robert, *The Siege of London*, Dent, 1946
Hubert, Maria and Andrew, *A Wartime Christmas*, Sutton Publishing, 1995
Isaacs, Susan, *Evacuation Survey*, Pluto, 1985
McCarthy, Tony, *War Games*, Queen Anne Press, 1989
Turner, E.S., *The Phoney War on the Home Front*, Michael Joseph, 1961

Articles:

Burnham, Roy, 'I'm No Nigger Minstrel', *Men Only*, September 1941
Orwell, George, 'As I Please', *Tribune*, December 1946
Spender, Stephen, 'Christmas Day at Station XIY', *Fire and Water*, Firestorm Publications, 1992

Magazines and Periodicals, 1939–45:

Artist, The
Beano
Columbia and Parlophone Record Guide, The
Daily Express
Daily Mirror
Good Housekeeping
Guider, The
His Master's Voice Record Guide
Home Chat
Home Notes
Illustrated
Kentish Mercury
Landgirl
Melody Maker
Motor Cycling
Needlewoman & Needlecraft
News Chronicle
Picture Post
Radio Times
Scouter, The
Shaftesbury Magazine
Sporting Life
Stage, The
Stitchcraft
Sunday Dispatch
Times, The
Woman
Woman and Home
Woman's Own
Woman's Pictorial
Woman's Weekly

Index